Souvenirs of the Past

American History Imprints / American History Press

Franklin, Tennessee

www.Americanhistoryimprints.com

www.Americanhistorypress.com

ISBN 10: 0-9999999-99

ISBN 13: 999-0-9999999-9-0

Published August 2009

Note: This is an exact facsimile reprint of the original 1896 2nd Edition

Printed in the United States of America on acid-free paper

This book meets all ANSI standards for archival quality

William L. Baby

Souvenirs of the Past

With Illustrations

AN INSTRUCTIVE AND AMUSING WORK, GIVING A CORRECT
ACCOUNT OF THE CUSTOMS AND HABITS OF THE

Pioneers of Canada

AND THE SURROUNDING COUNTRY, EMBRACING MANY
ANECDOTES OF ITS PROMINENT INHABITANTS, AND
WITHAL AN ABSOLUTE CORRECT AND HISTORICAL
ACCOUNT OF MANY OF THE MOST IMPORTANT
POLITICAL EVENTS CONNECTED WITH THE
EARLY DAYS OF CANADA AND THE
TERRITORY OF MICHIGAN.

BY

William Lewis Baby

Windsor, Ontario, 1896.

Table of Contents

An Old Family Legend during the Conspiracy of Pontiac 1

The Destruction of W. Lyon McKenzie's Press 12a

Serving Jury Summons in 1829 13

The Old Family Compact—its origin, and what I know about it 35

The Hon. James Bâby—Obituary 58

Service on the Detroit Frontier during the Rebellion of '37 and '38 72

Visit of the Prince of Wales to Detroit in September, 1860 .... 89a

The Battle of Windsor, fought December 4, 1839 90

Prominent Men of Essex 116a

An Old Time Breeze on Lake Erie—Sailing in 1831 .. 117

Journey from Little York to Sandwich in 1827 ...... 122a

Navigation on Lake Ontario—1824 .... 125a

At School in St. Raphael's in 1825 .... 127a

The Runaway Slave 129

Journey to Little York (now Toronto) in 1833 140

Visit to Col. Talbot in 1841 148

An Unexpected Visit from an Old Schoolmate 156

Visit to the Village of Wickwimikong, Manitoulin Island 164

Thrilling Experience with an Indian Pilot 187

The Book Peddler 193

Visit to the Sault Ste. Marie 215

A Sketch Showing, Among Other Things, how the Bruce Mines in Algoma were discovered 224

Farming in this Canada of Ours, and how it was I became a Farmer 240

Twenty-two Years' Service in H. M. Customs 266a

Illustration Index 272

Book Index 274

This Second Edition respectfully dedicated to my numerous patrons by the Author.

William Bâby was born in the Duff-Bâby house, Sandwich Towne, on April 13, 1812. While reading this account, you will learn a great deal about family life in Essex County in the mid 1800s, and this house in particular. The Ontario Heritage Foundation (Ontario Heritage Trust) has declared the Duff-Bâby house a historic site and has carefully restored it for public viewing and enjoyment. Please take the time to benefit from a tour of the house and taking a walk in the footsteps of our past. Chiefs Tecumseh, Pontiac and Splitlog have all walked its halls, as have Generals Brock, Harrison, Hall and Colonel Proctor. One of these people may indeed be the ghost that is said to walk the halls today. The Duff-Bâby Mansion may be experienced on many levels, providing entertainment, discovery and pleasure for all its visitors.

This book takes place at the end of the period in Upper Canada's life referred to as "The Foundation of British Canada". This era ended in 1815, when the political groundwork for British Canada had been firmly established. At its conclusion, British Canada had a distinct dividing line, both literally and figuratively, between Canada and the United States, as the wars between Great Britain, The United States, France and the North American Indians had finally come to an end. The stories in this book continue with the next phase: "The Middle Period: Ships, Colonies and Commerce 1815 to 1867." It was a time for what is now the Province of Ontario to establish a "Canadian" (as interpreted as a lessening of dependence on British ways) political form of representative government. It was also the occasion for the development of a physical infrastructure, with great interest and energy being devoted to the establishment of roads and communities.

The Honorable Jacques Bâby and his brother François were the most powerful and influential people in the British Detroit region. Their status led to some serious concerns in the middle period, because the citizens of the Canadas wanted to abolish the British class system. The Bâby family represented this system, and were part of the

"Family Compact" who ruled at the time. The 1837
Rebellion destroyed this system forever, and initiated
many changes in the framework of society. Many of the
stories you will read in the text reflect on this era of our
country's growth. William in particular was a product of
his father's upbringing, and was an upper class gentleman
of wealth and importance. He tried a variety of methods
in order to preserver his wealth while prospering in the
community, and this narrative includes accounts of his
many ventures. For instance, the chapter entitled "An Old
Time Breeze…" shows his occasional lack of good
judgment as we read of the mutiny of his captain and
crew from his ship *Tecumseh* during its voyage from
Albertville to York.

The story "An Old Family Legend" gives the details of
how the Hon. Jacques Bâby was bribed by the British
government in order to turn in Chief Pontiac. In another
chronicle, we learn that William Bâby's father, Jacques,
was held captive in his own home during the War of
1812. General William Henry Harrison, who later

became the United States' "One Month" President, used the mansion as his headquarters while the United States briefly held Essex County as their own.

The Family Compact in Ontario, The Rebellion in 1837, and the housing of the prisoners in the windmills are other stories that will have you cheering for the residents of Essex County. William Bâby and his friends were important investors in the town of Olinda, the industrial heartland of the area as well as the largest community in Essex County in its day. It is now a deserted town, as one can learn from the entertaining book "Tour Olinda: Essex Counties only Ghost Town."

In this volume you will read the unique story of the Jesuit Pear tree, located on the front lawn of the Bâby house, and relish the account of how the Bâby family protected a man (Andrew) from the bounty hunters in "The Runaway Slave." In "A Journey to Little York," we meet the eccentric old Colonel Talbot during an encounter that lends us a glimpse into William Bâby's true motivations. As the narration takes us to York, we learn

how William's brothers launched the Mackenzie
Rebellion, in "The Destruction of W. Lyon McKenzie's
Press." Not to be forgotten is the description of "The
Visit of the Prince of Wales to Detroit in September
1860."

Souvenirs of the Past, first printed in 1896, includes a
variety of first hand accounts from an earlier period of our
Canadian history, a time vastly different from our own in
many ways. These short stories (and accompanying
sketches) are presented in a readable, enjoyable format
with unforgettable characters and scenes from the past.
With a little imagination, you will find yourself
witnessing and participating in the world of William Bâby
as though you were there yourself!

Chris Carter
Author and Historian, Essex County

INTRODUCTION

Publisher's note:

With the recognition of the historical importance of the
stories contained in this book to the history of Essex
County, and indeed Canada in general, Chris Carter has
done us all a favor. Many of these accounts contained
herein are unique, and cannot be found in any other
format, especially those written from a first hand
prospective. We are delighted to play a part in reprinting
the second edition of William Bâby's book, a version
chosen for its extra stories and narration. An index has
also been added to make it easier for the reader to locate
the characters and places mentioned in the book.

David Kane
Publisher

SOUVENIRS OF THE PAST.

AN OLD FAMILY LEGEND DURING THE CONSPIRACY OF PONTIAC.

Pontiac, the renowned Ottawa chief and warrior, came down from his camping ground on the Isle au Pêche, (fishing island in French), situated immediately at the head of the Detroit River. From time immemorial Isle au Pêche, was noted for its fishing qualities. The deep and pure waters of the Detroit River (the spawning nurseries of the noted whitefish) were so attractive that on reaching the shallow waters of Lake St. Clair they refused its allurements and consequently congregated in tens of thousands around this island, and the feeding and gravelly shores of charming Belle Isle. No wonder that Pontiac loved this island. Pontiac proceeded to visit his old friend and trader, Jacque Duperon Bâby, and found him at his store adjoining his house, situated on the bank of the Detroit River, where Bâby and Hanrahan's liquor store now stands. It was a low log building eighty feet long by twenty feet wide, clap-boarded, and contained several rooms in a row, and was almost opposite Fort Pontchartrain, then situated on what is now called Griswold street, City of Detroit, close to the river bank.

"Sit down," said Bâby.

Pontiac, looking suspiciously at him, reluctantly took a seat before the log fire.

"They tell me," remarked the chief, "that those red coats have offered to give you a basket full of silver if you will betray me into their hands?"

"How foolish that would be," said his friend. "I, who make a living by trading with you and your tribes. As a proof of my friendship we will smoke the pipe of peace," handing him a four-pound plug of tobacco, in the shape of a huge cigar, and a clay pipe.

Pontiac, seizing his tomahawk, and pointing to its head, said, "Here is my pipe," (and the handle formed its stem), lit and smoked it. After their smoke his host remarked: "It's a long walk to the island to-night; there are my buffalo skins; use them and sleep before the fire and see if I betray you in the morning, but before going to bed have some supper. Theresa?" (a black negress) Bâby called. "She has gone to bed," Mrs. B. replies. "What is wanting?" "A bowl of bread and milk for Pontiac." "I will fetch it myself," Mrs. B. replies, and enters with a silver tray, a large china bowl, a loaf of bread and a silver spoon. "Good squaw, Bâby; many paupooses?" Pontiac asks. "Yes," and Bâby holds up both hands twice, counting twenty.

"Big camp," exclaims Pontiac, smokes his tomahawk pipe after supper in silence, makes his bed of buffalo skins and goes to sleep with his feet to the fire. The next morning Pontiac gets his breakfast with Mackinac toast, (slices of bread, dipped in batter and fried in lard or butter, and when done to a turn, can be served on a napkin without soiling), pork steaks, and a bowl of coffee, and tells him that he won't see him again for two weeks—squaw sick and too far from home.

At this moment Mrs. B. appears and shaking hands with the chief, said, "Good-bye, Pontiac; remember me to your squaw, and when you return to see us bring me six marten skins, dressed, for a boa, and a beaver skin for my bonnet. Here are eight yards of blue cloth for a frock and leggins, a red blanket, and twelve yards calico for her, two shirts, a double handful of assorted glass beads and a silver brooch (the size of a saucer) to wear on her breast, with the profile of old King George III. stamped upon it. Accept this also from me," handing him a silver box with six flints, tinder and a steel for striking fire. If she had left a $300 gold repeater and the silver box to choose from, he would have left the watch and taken the silver box. "If that is not enough my husband will pay you the difference." Pontiac gives a grunt and wraps them in the blanket, says "bon jour" and leaves.

Jacque Duperon Bâby, his majesty's Indian agent, Indian trader and farmer, and his wife, Susanne Reaume, were princely in their gifts to this monarch of forests, prairies, lakes and streams, and no wonder they sought his protection and favor, for Parkman, the great American historian, relates the following exhibition of his power over his followers—page 258, Vol. 1.

A few young Wyandottes were in the habit of coming, night after night, to the house of Bâby to steal hogs and cattle. The latter complained of the theft to Pontiac, and desired his protection. Being at that time ignorant of the intercourse between Bâby and the English, Pontiac hastened to the assistance of his friend, and, arriving about nightfall at the house, walked to and fro among the barns and enclosures. At a late hour he distinguished the dark forms of the plunderers stealing through the gloom. "Go back to your village, you Wyandotte dogs," said the Ottawa chief. "If you tread again on this man's land, you shall die." They slunk back abashed, and from that time forward the Canadian's property was safe. The Ottawas had no political connection with the Wyandottes, who speak a language radically distinct. Over them he could claim no legitimate authority; yet his powerful spirit forced respect and obedience from all who approached him.

1. Tradition related by M. Francis Bâby, of Windsor, U. C., the son of Pontiac's friend, who lived opposite Detroit, upon nearly the same site formerly occupied by his father's house. Though Pontiac at this time assumed the

attitude of a protector of the Canadians, he had previously, according to the anonymous diary of the siege, bullied them exceedingly, compelling them to plough land for him and do other work. Once he forced them to carry him in a sedan chair from house to house to look for provisions.— Parkman, 259, vol. 1.

The same morning Bâby said to Susanne, his wife, after breakfast: "I will cross the river in my canoe and see Major Gladwin" (commanding the fort). He then crossed the river and approaching, meets a soldier with two pails of water on a wooden yoke across his shoulders, addresses him as follows: "My man, tell Major Gladwin that Jacque Duperon Bâby wants to see him. Have him send me the countersign to pass the sentry. Here is half a crown for you and be quick." The message is soon delivered and the soldier returned, breathing in Bâby's ear, "Silence." Approaching the sentry he is accosted with, "Who goes there?" "A friend," he answers. "Advance, friend, and give the countersign." When close to the sentry he answers, "Silence." "Pass on," said the sentry, and he hastens to the major's quarters, gives the knocker (a brass rampant lion) three loud claps, which bring the major to the door. "Hello, Bâby, is this you? Glad to see you; come in, make yourself comfortable. It's rather too early to drink, but a glass of old Jamaica will do no harm after paddling across the river." "Never refuse a good thing in moderation," replied Bâby. They take a horn and Bâby says: "Well, Gladwin, what's the news?" "D—n bad; these infernal savages pester the life out of us, with their bows of poisoned arrows. We can't leave the fort but they are dogging us; at night they are in their camps in the thick woods and are quiet; but the worst of all, to-morrow we'll be out of provisions."

"What news from that cut-throat, Pontiac?" "He paid me a visit last night," said Bâby. "Smoked the pipe of peace with me. My wife gave him his supper and he slept in my buffalo skins in my dining room with his feet to the fire. He was up bright and early, got his breakfast, and by this time is opposite the head of Isle au Cochon," (now Belle Isle). "Good! you are a brick!"

"See here, Gladwin, to-morrow night set a lantern near the water plank," (two stakes driven in the bed of the river and a stout rung passed through them to support the plank, and extending into the river to the depth of four feet,) "and at half-past 12 sharp, look out for me with six canoes loaded with pork, corn meal and beef. Have your soldiers ready at the gate with empty casks to unload the meal, and I will make three trips in succession before daylight. Will bring a five-gallon keg of old Jamaica, five gallons of old port and five gallons of Madeira. Tell your men to use all precaution and be as quick as possible. Good day, Gladwin; I must hasten back home and to work. Keep up your courage, old boy, and all's well." Bâby shakes hands and hurriedly leaves him. Gladwin returns to his fireplace and in a musing mood says in a smothered voice, "What a brave and noble Frenchman—and a Loyalist at that." Recrossing the river, Bâby, calling his hands together, said, "Boys," (he had thirty slaves, twenty men and ten women), "you have your hands full." (He worked a large farm, 1,000 acres in size, and about 200 acres in cultivation, now all built over by the City of Windsor.) "Pompy," to his foreman, "to-morrow by sundown have forty hogs killed and dressed, ten head of fat cattle the same, and sixty bags of corn meal; put two quarters of beef and three hogs and six bags of meal in each canoe." As agreed upon at 12:30 at night the lantern gave its dim light at the water plank; six canoe-loads of provisions were dumped in a hurry and returned till all was over by daylight. And Gladwin thanked him, saying, "England will not forget you," and Bâby answered him, "I know it; and when you want my services hereafter, suspend from the flagstaff the white ensign of St. George, and I will respond." The following summer, not long afterwards, he noticed the cross of St. George and crossed over the river and met Gladwin in sore tribulation, and asked him, "What's up?" and Gladwin replied, "I am expecting a vessel up from Fort Erie and she is overdue some three weeks, loaded with arms, provisions and men for my garrison. Can you find a way for me to get news of her and ascertain if she is liable to be attacked before reaching here?" and Bâby replied, "I have traders all through the country on both sides of the river and lake (Erie), and I will instruct them to give me the news of her, if seen, and in the meantime discover the attitude of the Indians and report to you the

result of my inquiries in forty-eight hours from now.   Farewell."   Returns home in his canoe and on his arrival there
asks his slave Therese, "Where is Laframboise?" (his
trader).   She answers, "he is in the barn knitting a seine."
"Tell him I want him immediately."   Laframboise makes
his appearance, removes his capuchon rouge and says, "me
voici monsieur, que voulez vous?"   "I want you to get
ready immediately," said B., "and take with you in your
canoe fishing twine, fish-hooks, tobacco and pipes, glass
beads, etc., etc.   I will make the assortment for you to
trade with the Indians.   You will at once proceed in your
canoe to the mouth of the Riviere au Canard; you will as-
cend it on one side for two miles, and return on the other.
Keep your eyes open, and report to me by to-morrow
night what you have seen.   Comprenez vous, prend
garde?"   Exit the trader, and in an hour he is off.   On
the following day at midnight he reports.   "I followed your
instructions, sir, and the Indians knowing me as a trapper
allowed me to enter among their tribes, and I found Indians encamped on both sides of the river; Wyandottes,
Hurons and Pottowattomies, engaged in making bows and

arrows of young hickory wood; the squaws were twisting strips of deerskin, and using the inner bark of elm for the bow strings, and others tieing strips of wild turkey feathers on the arrows to guide their flight, with a split to insert the poisoned flint barb, tying them neatly and firmly, with the finest thread of the raccoon gut. As I was leaving I entered a camp where an old squaw was engaged in dyeing porcupine quills in various colors for embroidering moccasins, etc. Seating myself beside her, I pulled from my coat pocket a handful of assorted beads, a pound of tobacco and a pipe, a paper of needles and pins, and handing them to her I said in Indian, 'You appear to be very busy in your camps; what is it all about.' 'We expect,' she replied, 'to soon see a vessel of red coats come up the river, and we are going to capture her when she passes Turkey Island.' Voila tout mon maitre." "Good," said Bâby, "Here is a guinea from Major Gladwin for you," and Bâby gives Gladwin the information he sought for so anxiously within the promised time. It was correctly concluded from his information that a large force of Indians armed with bows and arrows would assemble ·

near Turkey Island and would make a night attack on the
vessel on her way up. This news was conveyed to Gladwin, who in turn notified the captain, while the vessel was
anchored in the stream immediately opposite to that island.
In the dead of the night the crew and all on board, behind
the bulwarks, impatiently waiting and ready for the attack,
observed a flotilla of fifty or more canoes stealthily creeping along the rushes. Suddenly the attack was made upon
the schooner, but so effectually were they received with
grape, cannister and musketry that they were swept from
the waters. (See Parkman, page 289, vol. 1.) And on
the following day the vessel hoisted sail and reached the
fort in safety with an abundance of provisions, was unloaded and returned for another trip.

THE DESTRUCTION OF W. LYON McKENZIE'S PRESS.

1824.—This proved an eventful year for Canada.

It was while attending school kept by Mr. Patfield that I was witness to an occurrence that at the time produced a sensation not easily to be described and sealed the fate of Canada—i. e., the destruction of the printing press of the notorious colonial advocate newspaper, published by Mr. W. Lyon McKenzie. As was our school boy custom in those days, a favorite pastime was bathing, not, I'm sure, for cleanliness alone, but more for the fun of the thing and cooling off. At that time the only approaches for steamers or vessels were two wharves extending some 200 yards into the bay, and respectively owned by the late Wm. Allan, H. M. Customs, foot of Jarvis, and one Cooper, foot of Young street. It was on the former place when, about 4 p. m., I, with a lot

of other scamps, had repaired for our wonted amusement
and stripped to the buff. Our usual way was to take a run
of fifteen or twenty yards and with a bound leap into the
water head first, feet first if we could, but sometimes couldn't
and struck the water back or belly first, the latter producing
by no means an agreeable sensation. Emerging from one
of these daring feats, I observed my two brothers, Charles
and Raymond, with James King and Charles Heward, descending the road on a full run to the wharf, and pitching
what they had in their arms into the bay and hastily return
to McKenzie's office on top of the hill. Aware that something extraordinary was in progress and quickly dressing
myself, I soon discovered they were the unfortunate types
of the Colonial Advocate (McKenzie's) they were putting an end to. Following them up, I discovered the office
(part of McKenzie's dwelling) completely gutted, and an
anxious crowd suddenly gathered together, and impressed
with this most extraordinary, outrageous and unlawful act.
A most ridiculous scene it was to see the foreman, who had
taken refuge in the privy, through the door of which was cut

out a half moon, and at each time he dared to peep through it he was peppered with a hand full of type.

The mischief being over, the band of outlaws assembled together armed with bludgeons (no doubt anticipating an attack from the enraged inhabitants), walked off the field in good order. And well do I remember after secreting their arms they repaired to my father's house, whom they found seated at his dinner table, and with his usual hospitality invited them to be seated, and, the wine decanters passing pretty freely, they broached the subject to him through Jas. King, student at law under the Hon. I. H. Boulton. Listening to him attentively until he had finished (suppressing the names of the parties), he was not a little surprised to find that my father disapproved of it in very measured terms, denouncing it as a cowardly and blackguard act.

The parties implicated in this outrageous affair were Peter McDougall, merchant; Samuel Jarvis, Indian agent; I. Proudfoot, of the Upper Canada Bank; Charles Richardson, law student; W. Campbell, law student; Charles and

Raymond Bâby, James Strachan, James King, William Lyons and if any others I have forgotten them.

McKenzie immediately returned to Canada, from which he had fled for debt, instituted an action for damages and recovered a large amount, costing my poor father $2,000 for the shares his two hopeful sons were obliged to pay.

It may as well be stated here that this unlawful act was, in the eyes of many, justifiable from the fact that the most villainous calumnies affecting the characters of Canada's most honorable men were scattered broadcast through the medium of this sheet, not only of the living, but of the dead.

SERVING JURY SUMMONS IN 1829.

In the month of May, 1829, and for many years previous, my worthy uncle, the late William Hands, might well have been called the Governor of Canada West, for apart from being collector of customs, postmaster, treasurer and register, and holding other offices of minor importance, he was sheriff of the western district, which embraced the counties of Essex, Kent and Lampton, covering a territory of 2,817 square miles. I was then sojourning in the picturesque old town of Sandwich. The youngest son of Mr. William Hands, Felix, was acting as deputy sheriff and was entrusted with the service of summoning the jury for the court of assizes (then held but once a year at Sandwich), and by his earnest request I was persuaded to assist and accompany him in the service. It was necessary to send a portion of these summonses by way of the St. Clair river, to be left at Sarnia for the northern division of the district, and as a steamer (the Superior) was about to leave Detroit on her first trip

to Sault Ste. Marie, I was commissioned by Felix to proceed to Detroit and send them by her.   To cross the Detroit river in those days was not accompanied with the
same ease and facility that it is done nowadays.   At that
time no person dreamed of such a place as the town of
Windsor, in fact, John G. Watson, merchant, Chas. Jeannette, Francois Bâby, Vital Ouellette, Daniel Goyeau
and Francois Pratt were the only settlers in it, who lived
on the banks of the river as simple farmers.   On the
Ouelette farm was an inn kept by Pierre St. Armour (on
the spot where the British American now stands), who
kept a ferry, i. e., log canoe No. 1.   Francois Labalaine, an
old and honorably discharged servant of the Hudson Bay
Company, who lived nearly opposite the residence of the
late Francois Caron on the Jeannette farm, and whose
old home is still standing on the bank of the river, ran
the other ferry, that is, log canoe No. 2.   The fixed
price for the round trip was twenty-five cents.*   Instead of

---

*The staunch steamers of the Detroit, Windsor & Belle Isle Ferry
Company make this trip through one foot of solid ice in fifteen
minutes, and every comfort is provided by Messrs. Campbell, Avery
and Clinton for their passengers.

a bell or whistle, Madame Labalaine had suspended over
the door a tin horn, exactly four feet long, which she
blew to call old Francois' attention to impatient passengers. These places were called by the habitants "La
Traverse," that is, the crossing. Labalaine's canoe was
his home, for, being severely afflicted with rheumatism,
he was unable to get in or out of it without assistance,
and a rare treat it was to listen to the old chap's stories
of his exploits among the Indians and half-breeds of the
Northwest Territory, as he leisurely paddled you over,
and landed you wherever it suited his greater conveni-
ence, either at the foot of Woodward avenue, Griswold,
Shelby or Cass streets. Crossing over with Francois and
landing at Griswold street, the first person I met was
my uncle, James Abbott, who was then the postmaster
for the City of Detroit and agent for the Southwest Fur
Company, with the famous John Jacob Astor as President. The population of Detroit at that time was 2,222.
Now, 1894, 250,000. James Abbott was acting as steamboat agent. To him I entrusted the summons to be forwarded to Sarnia by the steamer, and returned to Sand-

wich by log canoe No. 2. Although I had but little experience in roughing it in the bush I had an idea that in
undertaking this long journey I required suitable clothing and equipped myself accordingly. Not so with my
good cousin, Felix, who was tricked out with a black
silk velvet cap, with a gold band, a nicely fitting blue
cloth jacket, slashed with braid, tightly fitting black kersi-
mere pantaloons strapped over a pair of patent leather
shoes, in fact, he looked more like a lady's page than
the servitor of His Majesty's jury summons. Our tan-
dem team and dog cart being ready, we threw our sad-
dles and bridles into the tail end of it, and then started,
a jolly pair, on our peregrinations. Leaving Sandwich,
our road was along the Detroit river bank, which we followed to its source, Lake St. Clair, and soon arrived at
what was then called La Vallé's Point. The road here
was a heavy, sandy one and as La Vallé kept a tavern, it offered a good pretext to tarry and smile, which
we did. We then continued our journey along the shore
of the lake, arriving in the evening at the Puce (Flea)
river. A more appropriate name could not be given it,

which we learned to our cost, for on turning into bed we were so besieged by the nocturnal disturbers that we were soon glad to turn out of it, fly to our cart, which we filled with hay, and in it passed the night comfortably, at least flealess. Still following the lake shore brought us to Stony Point, where an inn was kept. I think a more appropriate name would be caravanserie, for if in the east that name implied a place of rest and safety for the weary traveller, surely this one answered the same purpose in Canada West. Not that I would for a moment lead you to believe that there was danger from highway robbers; far from it, as Pierre Langlois, Jacques Parent and Dominique Pratt would attest, who were the mail carriers that transported the mail from Sandwich to Little York (now Toronto) either on foot or on horseback, every alternate week from 1820 to 1835, and who never dreamt of danger in that way. But there was danger in other ways, namely, the horrid condition of the roads. At the time I am writing about and for many years thereafter, the tide of emigration from the eastern to the western states was through Upper Canada, through which a stage route had been established. Starting from Detroit, after crossing the river, this road wound itself eastward along the river bank and Lake St. Clair shore, sometimes flanked by water on one side and marsh or forest on the other; again a prairie was to be encountered and anon an almost interminable forest through part of which a corduroy road was constructed, between Chatham and Hamilton at intervals. It consisted simply of huge logs thrown together without a covering, to keep horses and wagons from disappearing below. On arriving at the caravanserie kept by my old friend, Francois Chauvin, you very abruptly left the lake shore road and struck the prairie. Often have I been amused to see starting from this spot two or three four-horse stage coaches with from eight to twelve passengers in each coach. The driver, on approaching the prairie, would pause and survey closely the place before him. Now, it was not exactly what he saw, but what he could not see, that appalled him, for well he knew from sad experience that there were holes and morasses sufficient to ingulf him and his four-in-hand out of sight if he was unfortunate

enough to fall into one. But nerved with the stimulant
of various horns of "tangle-leg," freely supplied him by
his passengers, and whirling his 20-foot lash over his head,
which emitted a sound like a pistol-shot, he boldly made
for it. For what? Of course for what he could not see
—one of the aforesaid holes. Thus entrapped, there was
no help for the driver but to unload his passengers, who,
seizing the snake fence-rails surrounding the caravanserie
and using them as pries, succeeded in releasing the coach
from one hole to be precipitated into another, and thus
was the passage continued until the banks of the river
Thames, some twelve miles distant, were reached, where,
the road being passable, the travellers unshouldered their
arms (the rails). Francois Chauvin's inn (or caravanserie, I will persist in calling it) was popularly known as
the "Goose" tavern. In fact, this aquatic bird was so in-
geniously prepared in various ways by mine host that it
constituted the principal and standing dish for breakfast,
dinner and supper. The surrounding inhabitants found
a lucrative occupation in propagating geese for the
"Goose" tavern's table, and feather beds. Before bidding

adieu to my old friend Chauvin, it would not be out of
place to narrate what became of him . Shortly after the
Great Western Railroad was established, which event
happened in 1854, I believe, his occupation of keeping
the "Goose" tavern was gone.   He then took to farming, and instead of raising geese, began to raise corn to
fatten hogs, and for many years his efforts as a farmer
were crowned with success.   But, unfortunately for Chauvin, a brace of cockneys came down from Chatham one
fine autumn day to have a day's quail shooting.   They
flushed a bevy of quail in Chauvin's cornfield, in which
the corn was eight or ten feet high, and let fly the contents of their four barrels, two of which poured into Francois' eyes, making, as it were, a "dead shot."   Chauvin
at the time was perched on a rider of his snake fence at a
point where it was impossible for the huntsmen to see
him.   He recovered from this eventually with the loss of
his eyes, but the shock was too great for him, and in a
short time afterwards, in a fit of desperation, he put an
end to his miserable existence by hanging himself in his
barn.   Nor can I bid a final adieu to this prairie without
alluding to another incident which occurred to me some
years after 1836.

My friend, Harry Jones, then Crown Land Agent at
Chatham, made a wager with some friend that we could

bag a certain number of ducks (25 brace) by a certain time, and for that purpose we started for the prairie at Janette's Creek, where resided an acquaintance of ours, Mr. T., by whose invitation we made his home our headquarters. Immediately in front of T.'s house the prairie road commenced. At that point it entered a slough or quagmire, which, being covered with water, proved a terror to the western emigrants, who no sooner entered it than they found it impossible to budge without additional animal power. Appeals would therefore be made to our friend, who kept a yoke of oxen always ready for the occasion. T., for a certain sum (five dollars) would, in a very reluctant manner, turn out his team from behind a shed where they were concealed and extricate the conveyance from its difficulty. Five, ten, fifteen and even twenty dollars was often a day's compensation for this kind of work. The country surrounding Janette's Creek then was nearly covered with water and afforded magnificent sport to the duck and muskrat hunter. It was to complete the number of ducks we were to shoot on our wager that led me to do the following hazardous and most foolish act. I jumped into a trapper's canoe or dugout, which was about twelve feet long and twelve or fifteen inches wide. Seating myself in the center of it, that being the only way it would carry my weight, I started down stream. After paddling a mile or so in the center of the creek, which was about eighty yards in width and twelve or fifteen feet deep, I observed five wood-ducks coming towards me. As they were about passing over me I prepared to give them the contents of a double-barrelled gun which was borrowed from James Perrier. Following them with my aim, I discharged both barrels at the flock. Of course, what might have been expected did occur, i. e., the upsetting of the canoe in the twinkling of an eye. Whether my shot took effect I could not tell, but one thing certain was I found myself at the bottom of the creek, twelve feet below the surface, encumbered with my gun, overcoat, shot-bag and a pair of boots coming well up to my hips. How I managed to reach the surface puzzles me now, but I did so and found myself some ten or fifteen feet from my canoe, to regain which I made a desperate effort. Upon reaching it I found it bottom side up, and immediately set to work to right it. This task was accomplished only by great physical exertion. I then threw my gun into the canoe, and seizing one end of it, pushed it before me. On reaching the edge of the rushes I became exhausted. My strength failed me. The last ray of hope appeared to be fading away, and the thoughts of a watery grave flashed vividly across my excited brain. As I was about to give up the contest I found, to my infinite relief, that I could touch bottom by standing on tip-toe. In this position my mouth was just out of water, which enabled me to recover my breath. As soon as I regained sufficient strength I hauled my boat ashore, fully determined never more to shoot ducks in Janette's Creek from a trapper's canoe. I find I have been digressing from my subject and will therefore say, in the language of my polite countrymen, "Revenons a nos moutons."

The year Felix and I travelled this road the season was comparatively dry. The road was in fair condition, so, with the assistance of a guide, we got along very well. After leaving the "Goose" tavern, the next stopping place

was at Narcisse Dauphin's inn, located near the banks of
the Thames. Here we were kindly received by the worthy host and hostess and regaled with a well served meal,
delightfully enhanced by being waited upon by their
charming daughters, who, it affords me pleasure to say,
are now all comfortably settled in life and honored members of society. From Dauphin's we followed the banks
of the Thames until we arrived at John Goss' House of
Entertainment, the former residence of W. McCrae, M.
P., four miles below Chatham, where we spent the night.
The next morning we reached Chatham at 8 o'clock. If
my memory serves me right three squatters comprised the
population of this place at that time, which was then covered with a heavy forest of beech, maple, walnut and various other kinds of timber; these were H. Chrysler, blacksmith; Israel Evans, who operated a horse-power card-
ing machine, and P. P. L., our kinsman, on whom we
greatly relied for proper information regarding the manner and way of serving our jury summons in the southern part of the district, then almost completely a forest.
What P. P. L.'s particular occupation was he scarcely knew

himself, but generally he was ready for everything that turned up. Approaching his log house, situated on the banks of the Thames, we observed in front of the door this illustrious individual engaged in the interesting occupation of milking his cow.   He was seated on a three-legged stool.   Between his legs, which were thrust under the animal, sat the milk pail.   A bonnet rouge, jauntily worn, adorned his head, while his black clay pipe, grasped firmly by his well set teeth, emitted its gentle vapors, which he appeared to offer up on high as incense for the perfect happiness he enjoyed here below.   A buckskin shirt encircled his shoulders and loins, while blue cloth breeches faced in the seat and knees with large patches of deerskin, covered his nether limbs, the extremities of which supported a pair of "souliers de boeuf," or unfinished tanned leather boots.

P. P. L. was a philosopher, pure and simple, and nothing under heaven seemed to disturb the perfect equanimity of his mind and temper.   As an instance, my brother Charles, the previous winter, left Sandwich for Little York with his horse and sleigh, and encountered a terrific snow

storm before reaching Chatham and arrived at L.'s house
at eight or nine o'clock in the evening. The usual hos-
pitalities and warm reception was given him by mine
host, and no one in Canada could do it more gracefully.
Charles felt solicitous about his horse and inquired where
he was to be kept, whereupon P. P. L. instructed his
eldest boy to show him where the stock, consisting of a
cow and a yearling calf were wintered. To his dismay
and consternation he was led to a stack of marsh hay
into which a stake had been driven, and to this stake his
horse was secured by means of the lines, and covered
with a buffalo skin, left to its fate. There was not much
sleep for Charles that night and daylight found him
searching for his horse, which was attended with some
difficulty, as everything was covered with a mantle of snow
to a depth of two feet. The outlines of the stack, however, were visible and approaching the lee side of it, he
encountered a sight which provoked a smile. There he
beheld a row of fowls perched upon the animal's back,
doubtless attracted there by the warmth of the heavy buffalo skin with which the horse had been covered.   On

"DE STACK WAS GOOD FOR HIM, AND DE BLANKET, TOO."

complaining to the host of the bitter suffering the horse must have endured, the quiet response was: "De stack was good for him and de blanket too." Mr. P. P. L. received us with his usual courteous manner and advised us to leave our conveyance with him and proceed on horseback, as the roads were not opened for wagons, excepting along the banks of the Thames, and informed us that we would have to strike at different points through the woods and take the trails. Bidding him adieu we left with the promise of seeing him in a few days. Our route was along the banks of the Thames, until we reached the town line between Harwich and Howard. By taking this line we struck the Ridge road some nine miles distant, now Ridgetown, where the country was more or less settled. It is impossible for me to describe this town line. Imagine, if you can, an opening through a dense and heavily timbered forest, nine miles in length and sixty-six feet wide. Along this line trees from two to six feet thick were felled by dextrous axemen as close to each other as possible. The cutting was usually done in the summer months. Every branch and leaf was left upon the trees to add fuel to the flames when fired.   This vague description gives but a slight idea of it. To penetrate this line was quite impossible, so after a short consultation Felix decided to take one side of the line and I the other, which was traversed by swails and swamps in endless variety and covered with from one to four feet of water. It was decided to give a yell or an Indian "war whoop" to identify our locality. After penetrating some distance I was not surprised at hearing a yell from Felix, with the exclamation, "I can get no further." He had encountered a prostrate patriarch of the forest in the shape of an oak some five feet in diameter, over which his horse was struggling to clear himself, encumbered with his rider. Dismounting upon the oak, and taking a survey around him, he exclaimed: "What's to be done?" "Tie your pants and boots over your head," I replied, "and leg it." To do this, however, when the mosquitoes were as thick as the leaves on the trees, was not to be thought of, so, after a few more desperate efforts the horse was made to straddle and tumble over the oak. Of course, my way was no better than my companion's.

At length we both found it necessary to proceed on foot, leading our horses as best we could through this trackless forest. When we left our friend L. we expected to get through to the ridge by noon, but did not accomplish this task until seven o'clock in the evening, at which hour we stumbled upon a welcome clearing (the first one since leaving the banks of the Thames) belonging to Jonathan C., a squatter, I believe, situated about the spot where the town of Ridgetown now stands, with a population of 2,000 inhabitants. I'll venture to say a more bedraggled, forlorn pair of riders, with their sorry looking steeds, were never seen in this Canada of ours. On asking friend C. if he could keep us for the night, he replied, "Certainly, if you can rough it, but you don't look like folks accustomed to our way of grubbing." Now the terrors and escapes experienced on that town line were still fresh in our minds, added to which was the certainty of not reaching another halting place for ten or fifteen miles, so we quickly rejoined: "Oh, anything will do." To our great relief this squatter had a small stack of oats, and, fastening our jaded and fam-

ished horses to a sapling, we served them with a bounteous supply.   In attending to his horse Felix discovered
that one of the stirrups had been torn from the saddle
and occupied himself, with the assistance of Jonathan, in
making a substitute for it with strips of basswood bark,
whilst I thought it as well to proceed to the log hut to
see how the wind blew.   As I approached the hut a figure appeared at the open doorway, which proved to be
the amiable spouse of our worthy host, and well it was
that the breeze was light, otherwise it would have blown
all she had on from her back and left her as sailors say,
"under bare poles."   Her golden unkempt hair hung
loosely over her bare shoulders and, as she stood there
barefooted, she presented a singularly interesting picture.
Respectfully saluting her I asked her if she could get
supper for two.   She answered in the affirmative, and
asked me to walk in and take a seat, remarking at the
same time that victuals were scarce, and not much variety.
In fact, pork and buckwheat cakes was their standing
dish.   Seating myself on a block of wood next the wall
opposite the fireplace, I watched the busy housewife pre-

"AN INTERRUPTED SUPPER."

which she switched the little brat plump into the batter.
You are mistaken if you think this untoward event dis-
concerted her in the least. She simply seized the imp by
the nape of the neck and swashed the batter from its
naked limbs into the trough whence it came, and proceeded with her culinary art as if nothing had happened.
There was a grave consultation held outside of the hut
immediately after that between Felix and myself. He was
for total abstinence, and so was I if I could, but couldn't.
It proved that hunger was an uncompromising foe, and
proved the victor. (Sic semper tyrannus.) The buckwheat was utilized with sullen mood, and to our agreeable disappointment afterwards, we found our digestion
unimpaired. About nine o'clock that evening Mr. C. informed us that, when we felt inclined to rest he would
show us our sleeping apartment, which was in reality a
"lean to" or shed attached to his shanty—in fact a fowl
house. No floor or window marred its grandeur. The
furniture consisted of a bedstead constructed of strong
poles across which were strapped strips of basswood bark.
This formed our bed and bedding. I omitted to mention

pare the frugal meal. She seized from a shelf a large wooden trough which she quickly filled with buckwheat batter and then began to cut slices of salt fat pork for the fry. A large wooden crane was swung from the side of the chimney corner, suspended from which by a chain was a huge iron griddle and on this griddle, by means of a mequen (an Indian wooden spoon of large size) the batter was emptied. It took exactly four spoonfuls of batter to cover the solitary utensil. The fragrant odor arising from the hot iron, as it permeated the surrounding atmosphere of this rural retreat, acted like a charm, for in an instant a bevy of young urchins, followed by a half-starved cat and cur, came rushing in seeking what they could devour. The youngest, a yearling, I should judge, was clad in nature's garb (with the exception that a cloth was substituted in place of a fig leaf) and clung tightly to its mother's skirt, from which it could not be detached. I expected that some mishap would befall the little chap, and my expectations were shortly afterwards fully realized. Felix's sudden appearance at the open door caused the good lady to quickly turn round, in doing

"MENDING HIS TROUSERS."

the fact that Felix met with an accident in "brushing through the line." He tore his pants in a conspicuous place unhidden by his short jacket. It happened fortunately for him that one Schneider, a job tailor by trade, was residing with our host, and to him the pants were gladly entrusted for repairs. We then turned into our crib, while the tailor set to work. The picture of that evening is vividly before me. Seated on his wooden stool, with an empty flour barrel to serve as a table, a tin plate holding a pint of melted grease provided with a bit of rag for a wick, and with huge old-fashioned spectacles on his nose, sat the weary looking tailor as he plied his needle, enveloped in a cloud of mosquitoes. "Flies are pretty thick," remarked Felix. "Yaw," said Schneider; then shaking his head, he said, "Mosquito bite not mi." We were glad to tumble out of our rude bed next morning at daylight. Felix's horror can readily be imagined on finding a white patch as big as a saucer on the seat of his pants. The old chap had taken a piece of an old white cotton wheat bag with which to mend the pantaloons!

With great difficulty I succeeded in soothing Felix by assuring him that I would blacken the patch with a basswood brand, which I did after a fashion. Mounting our fresh horses and bidding our hospitable friends adieu, we cantered ten miles to our next stopping place. After serving the jurymen we returned to Chatham by the Raleigh, and not the Howard, town line, and proceeded to Sandwich by the old route. This was an exceptional portion of the old western district, and at that time recently settled. The older settlers in more favored parts were as comfortable and thriving as in any other portion of Canada. Sixty years have brought about a wonderful change in the affairs of the nation. To perform the same service now and reach this spot it is only necessary to step on board a dining room car at Windsor at 5 p. m. and if you feel inclined for a meal you can regale yourself with all the delicacies that the land affords, and, if you could persuade the conductor to slack for a moment, he would land you at 7:50 p. m. very near the spot where Felix encountered the old oak; in forty minutes more you could reach the C. place by travelling over as fine a gravel road and as well settled as is to be found in Canada. Or, by taking the Canada Southern road, with the same speed and comfort, you could arrive within a short distance of the same spot, which took us three days to accomplish, but would have to look in vain for anything belonging to Jonathan C., his amiable spouse, or Schneider, the job tailor.

THE OLD FAMILY COMPACT.

ITS ORIGIN AND WHAT I KNOW ABOUT IT.

Probably there is no subject relating to the history of Canada requiring more careful research and an honest and impartial pen to deal with than this very one. And I feel at a loss to account for my presumption in approaching it at all. In fact, the only excuse I can offer is this: I may consider myself as one of the few, and I am nearly safe in saying, (to borrow a phrase from Cooper), "The

Last of the Mohicans," linked to it and surviving, in Western Canada at any rate, and perhaps the only one who
has ever dared to raise a pen in its defense.

In dealing with this subject it will be necessary to turn
to the pages of the earliest history of Canada.

We must yield the palm to chivalrous France, whose
pioneers were the first missionaries, and following close
behind them, her nobles who first discovered and penetrated her vast domain from the Atlantic to the sources
of the Mississippi, aye, and on to the Rocky Mountains,
and what a living and imperishable monument to their
memory have they left, as we trace them step by step,
and the soul inspired sounds strike the ear of St. Laurent,
St. Thomas, St. Charles, Montmorenci, Quebec, Montreal, Lachine, Laprarie, St. Anne, Frontenac, Detroit, St.
Clair, Sault Ste. Marie, St. Ignace, Marquette, St. Paul,
St. Anthony, St. Louis, Baton Rouge, Nouvelle-Orleans,
and so many thousand others.

The French, then alone, with the consent (and often
without it), of the aborigines, occupied and governed the
country up to the time of the taking of Quebec—1759—

after which a new tide of affairs soon set in with an Anglo-Saxon race, and was followed, not many years later, with a further emigration from the colonies, now the eastern states, when, at the close of the revolutionary war, 1776, they declared their independence, the United Empire Loyalists, who had bravely contended for British supremacy, abandoned their homes and fled to Canada, to rest under old England's proud banner, and one they had so long fought and suffered for. The same may be said of the then territory of Michigan, when, in 1776, then Canada, it was, by treaty, ceded to the United States, and many of its oldest inhabitants for the same reason left it, losing their homes and large possessions, and crossed the Detroit river into Canada in order to live under the old English flag. One of these was the father of the writer.

There was no question then as to the loyalty and attachment to the crown, from Sandwich to Gaspé, of the inhabitants, which was more forcibly proved when, in a few years after, 1812, the American war was declared, and Canada had to fight and win her own battles with scarcely any help of Great Britain, then engaged in war on the continent with Napoleon I. Only four regiments served in Canada during this war. The peace of 1815 found Canada in the same position as it was in 1812 —had gained nothing, and lost nothing, but secured the confidence and attention of England.

Hitherto, but very little time was devoted by the thinly-populated country to its government, but the time now arrived when necessity demanded more active measures, and those entrusted with its formation wisely (as they believed) selected, as became necessary, those who had most distinguished themselves in the service and defense of their country for loyalty, education and integrity. Like all England's colonies, Canada suffered from British rule at first, and the greatest hindrance to the development and settlement of the country was the wretched and deplorable state of management of the public lands department. For instance: One-seventh of the provinces of Upper Canada was reserved for the support of the established church of England; the Canada Company formed in England had secured large tracts of the finest lands in Canada; Col. Talbot, a favorite of George the Fourth, was intrusted with several thousands of acres of land in the most favored part of the country, he retaining 100 acres out of every 200 for himself to pay him for his trouble in settling the country; all British officers, leaving the service, were entitled to draw 600 acres of land, and added to this, private individuals purchased large tracts. Thus it will be seen that the greatest obstacles presented themselves to the rapid settlement of the country, whilst our shrewd neighbors, the Americans, on the contrary, offered every inducement to fill up their vast territories to emigrants, offering them free homesteads and putting the upset price of $1.25 per acre of their best lands in their forest and western prairies, the latter yielding a return in one year to the industrious settler.

Although laboring under these disadvantages, still Canada slowly progressed, and, with a population far different to that in the United States, the English, Scotch and Irish, who left their homes with strong attachments to their native lands, were glad to find so welcome a reception. And being generally persons of more or less means, intelligence and education, and familiar with the modes of agriculture in the country they had left, the majority being tenants and farm servants, with a good sprinkling of merchants, tradesmen and merchanics; and, as a consequence, Ontario will surpass, if not compare favorably, with any portion of this continent, in its successful and progressive state of agriculture, education, intelligence and morality.

At the time I write of, say 1815 to 1835, a strong bond of friendship prevailed amongst the peaceable inhabitants generally, engendered and fostered, no doubt, by the difficulties, hardships and privations surrounding them in a new country. A man's word was as good as his bond. Robbery or murder was very seldom heard of. The mails, containing large sums of money, often carried on foot (it took exactly two weeks to go and return with the mail from Sandwich to Little York on foot), the roads being impassable for horses or vehicles throughout the length and breadth of the Province. It was a matter of frequent occurrence for the banks, merchants and others, to remit, by private hands, large sums of money—no receipt asked for or given. As an instance: In the month of November, 1834, on my way up from Quebec to Sandwich, I was compelled to lay over at Brantford, the roads being impassable for the stage. On the evening previous to my departure thence, I had retired to rest when, about midnight, I was aroused by the pressure on my shoulder of a heavy hand, and confronted my disturber, who, in a night cap and gown, with a lighted candle in one hand, and a package in the other, startled me a little. Apologizing for the intrusion, he asked me if my name was Bâby, and answering him in the affirmative, he introduced himself as Mr. Buchanan, the then British Consul at New York, stating that he was on his way to the Township of Adelaide to visit his son, who was settled there, and then proceed on to Sandwich, but finding the roads in such a state, abandoned the idea, and made up his mind to return home, and informing me that he had a package from the Commercial Bank at Little York for their agent at Windsor, James Dougall, Esq., and would I not take charge of it? I told him I would rather not, as I did not know how I was to get through myself; but, to get rid of him, I told him to pitch it into my trunk, which was open, and it would have to run the chances. After doing so, he bid me good-night, and retired. This package contained $25,000, so Mr. Dougall, the agent, told me when I delivered it to him, a month after.

On the following morning I left for London on foot, and my trunk to follow on the next stage, which did not reach me until three days after. If it were possible, I found the roads still worse westward, and made up my mind to float down the Thames from London, and as there was no boat to be had, I hired a carpenter, and, with my little engineering skill, built a kind of skiff with three boards, filled it half full of straw—the weather being very cold—threw my trunk, package and all into it, and amidst a flow of ice running six miles an hour, started on my voyage, paddling my own canoe and encouraged by a cheer from John Harris, treasurer, Wilson, Beecher and Stewart, lawyers of London, who stood on the bank watching my departure. A three days' run brought me to Gardener's mill dam, in Mosa, and landing above it, hired a mill hand to jump the skiff, trunk and package still in it though, over the mill race, which he successfully accomplished; but how, it puzzles me. Another two days' run brought me to within four miles of Chatham, when the river being blocked with ice, I landed and reached Chatham, on foot, the same day, all right.

It was not surprising that a feeling of security was felt throughout the land. A property qualification of £200 was required by the magistrates who were always chosen to serve on the grand juries, traveling often many miles to attend the assizes and quarter sessions, at their own expense and greatest inconvenience. This proved a good school in after years, for the changes which took place under the present form of responsible government, as none knew better the wants of the country than those who filled the ranks of our first municipal councils.

In 1822, or about that time, a noted character in the person of William Lyon McKenzie, and a man of untiring energy, ambition and unscrupulous audacity, occupied the public mind and started in Little York a paper called the "Colonial Advocate," which was destined to exercise a great influence on many of the quiet and hitherto peaceful inhabitants. Nothing was too vile, wicked, dishonest and unprincipled for this flaming sheet's attack upon those entrusted with the government, whom he styled the "family

compact." It proved a failure in a short time, and the
editor left the country for the United States to avoid the
bailiff's pressing demands.   Fortunately for him, an event
occurred which soon placed him on his legs again.   Some
dozen or more young dare devils, a few of whom were
sons of the traduced family compact, made an attack upon
his printing press, gutted it and threw the type, etc., into
the bay hard by, in broad daylight.   I was an eye witness
to it, though not a participant.   Nothing could have happened to him more opportunely.   He returned immediately
to the country, prosecuted and recovered full damages—
some $15,000 or $20,000—and started the paper with increased violence, defamation and bitterness.   At length,
finding his efforts for reform unavailable from the home or
Provincial Government, he raised the standard of rebellion
near Little York, was defeated, and again fled to the United
States, enlisted the sympathy of the American people, raised
a mob of Canadian refugees and, with the scum of Buffalo,
took possession of Navy Island, in Canadian waters, two
miles above the Falls of Niagara, and from which he was
dislodged by the capture of the American steamer "Caro-

line," which had been employed by him in furnishing artillery, arms, stores, etc., from Buffalo to the island, and was sent over the falls in a blaze, the bodies of several of the crew who were shot or could not escape, adding fuel to the flames.

When the rebellion was suppressed he remained in the United States, but such was his restless and turbulent will, that he soon got himself into trouble there, was tried for sedition, and imprisoned. After being released, he returned to Canada, where he died in 1863, I believe.

In reviewing the character and standing of those who were entrusted in carrying out the views of the British Government in those days, in many instances, as in all her colonial government, views entirely antagonistic to the colonists, and which they could not control, was this "family compact." Now, I hope I will not be considered egotistical in dealing with this subject. I find it necessary to commence with my own family. James Bâby, my father, in 1816, was appointed Inspector General of Upper Canada, and for what reason? In Morgan's work of "Celebrated Canadians," he states: "That when the war broke out, in 1812, he commanded the militia of the then western district now Essex, Kent and Lambton, and performed many services highly essential to the preservation of the Province.   The people had unlimited confidence in him. His merits had been so conspicuous during the war, his services so disinterested, his losses and privations so great, that the government was anxious to confer upon him some honor for his loyalty, and at the same time, some office, the revenue from which would in a measure compensate him for the Michigan and Indiana properties which he had abandoned—and he was appointed to the first high office within its gift, viz.: the office of Inspector General. So much for his merits.   Now for his reward.

To be sure, he enjoyed his salary of £750 per annum, and, when he died, he left a few hundred acres of wild land which he was entitled to for his services and the most of which he had inherited from his father, and not one of his children held a government appointment. Probably one of the most traduced and villified members of the Family Compact by this famous "Colonial Advocate" was the Archdeacon, afterwards Bishop Strachan.   Well do I remember this person when he kept the common grammar school in little Muddy York, and I was his pupil at 8 years of age. Even at that tender age, I had the most vivid recollection of his kindness, and unflinching integrity and liberality. For example: It was a rule of his school, on Saturday forenoon, to have the Church of England Catechism and the Bible taught, and the afternoon a holiday. There being several of his pupils Roman Catholics, he would say: "Boys, if you don't wish to stay, you can go home and learn your own Catechism," which we preferred not doing, as we would lose our playmates, and in consequence I know that one as well as my own. In the discipline of his school he invariably showed the strictest impartiality, and when any of his sons were implicated in mischief, they were always the first to suffer, and no light punishment as nowadays, but a good birch, and to the buff at that. I have often heard it said during the time of his life (he died in 1883), that he lived a luxurious and extravagant one for a bishop, that his table was sumptuous, his wines of the best quality, and he kept his carriage. This was all true to a certain extent, but I must not omit to

observe this about the latter, I never saw him once in it,
but I have met him repeatedly, and hundreds of times, on
foot, in town and country. To the liberal-minded Canadian there could be no reasonable objection to this; on the
contrary, by occupying the prominent position he did, as
one of the earliest pioneers, and obliged to entertain the
most distinguished strangers of Europe, such as clergymen,
soldiers, sailors, and noted travelers, and his distinguished
Canadian pupils as well, it was rather a source of pride
that he was one of them who could disabuse them of the
prevailing errors of the English people, who believed us to
be very little remote from savages. Now, as to the fulfill-
ment of his duties, no man could have performed his
mission with more faithfulness in such a wilderness as
Canada then was. When the cholera broke out in 1832,
and again in 1855, his labors were unceasing; night and
day was he to be met on foot in and out of town, visiting
the afflicted and administering the consolations of his religion. Again, in Morgan's sketches: Bishop Strachan
has ever been the friend of the poor, to his name has been
ascribed many benefits conferred upon them in the promo-

tion of education, and establishing institutions for the welfare of the old as well as the young. He has indeed merited all the love and affection which his people cherish for him. He is universally beloved and esteemed by his clergy and parishioners. But for him the celebrated Trinity College would not have been built in Toronto. Apropos of this college—when the Bishop visited England to procure aid for its erection, the writer was informed, on good authority, that he called upon the Duke of Wellington for aid in this laudable enterprise, but the Duke declined on the plea that he had no money to spare. The objection was surmounted by the Bishop informing him that he understood that he had £400 invested in the Welland Canal. The Iron Duke had forgotten this and replied, "Take it and welcome." It is not to be wondered at, that this man exercised so powerful an influence in this young country when from its extremest limits, the pulpit, the bench, and the bar, and other professions have been so ably and honorably represented in his pupils. We will hastily note some of them: First, would appear Sir John Beverly Robinson. Having known this man intimately, I consider it an honor and pride to bear this, my humble tribute, to his worth and character. It is difficult to say in which he most excelled—whether as a finished scholar, a jurist, a statesman, a patriot, or as an exemplary Christian, or polished and refined gentleman. I again quote from Morgan: "Born at Berthier, in Lower Canada, in 1791, the son of a U. E. Loyalist. He attained the high position of Attorney General at the early age of 22. He enjoyed the confidence of three successive governors—Sir Peregrine Maitland, Sir John Colborne and Sir Francis Bondhead. The thanks of the Legislature of Upper Canada was voted to him for the part he took in adjusting the financial difficulties of Upper and Lower Canada. He never once incurred the displeasure of his superiors, while, on the other hand, it was his good fortune to be honored with the express approbation of his sovereign on at least one occasion, and his public conduct especially elicited the approbation of colonial secretaries. On one occasion, he appealed to the three governors above named, then all living in England, to bear him witness that their approbation had not been obtained by the suppression of his

opinions or the surrender of his judgment. Belonging to
one of the few prominent families, who, having fought
under the British flag in the American war of independence, and took up their residence in Upper Canada, his
loyalty, as he himself said of U. E. Loyalists, was of no
doubtful origin, and when the war broke out in 1812, he
was one of a company of 100 volunteers who followed Sir
Isaac Brock in the expedition which led to the capture of
Detroit, and who penned its surrender to Brock in the old
Bâby house, still standing in Sandwich. During the whole
of his political career he was identified with the small official
party known as the Family Compact. They defended the
oligarchical system with a zeal fully proportioned to the
interest they had in maintaining it, and opposed the introduction of responsible government as if it had been an
over tried project under which British interests were sure
to suffer destruction. They opposed Lord Durham's mission as High Commissioner, and the Chief Justice, then
clothed with the judicial ermine, officially condemned the
report of that nobleman on the affairs of Canada. If he
erred in this particular, if time has proved that responsible

government was not pregnant with the danger that he supposed it was, but proved, to the contrary, the very thing suited for Canada, this much may, at least, be said, that he only showed the error of the entire official party in the Province, and that his error was the error of the times and a party, and that party systematically sustained by the British Crown.   Sir John B. Robinson is a picture of amiability and benevolence; he had a great flow of language and was a pleasant speaker; as a judge, his impartiality has never been impugned.   He received the honor of a baronetcy, having previously refused to accept a knighthood.   It will not be out of place here to insert the following correspondence as a proof of his honesty and disinterestedness:

Little York, Oct. 11th, 1823.

The Hon. James Bâby, Inspector General of Privy Council:

My Dear Sir—I must entreat you to say to the gentlemen who in company with you did me the honor to call upon me yesterday, that I have not been able to overcome my first impression upon the subject of their visit. I have no other reason for declining so gratifying a proof of the good opinion of my friends than that which I attempted to assign verbally, and I must rely upon your good nature for admitting it to be sufficient. I have never indeed objected to becoming a public character on our small stage, so far as it became necessary in the discharge of any public duty, but I have private feelings of repugnance to being placed in conspicuous situations, however flattering the occasion, which I will venture to beg of my friends to indulge when they interfere with no public service. Let me, however, beg of you to accept and convey my assurance that next to the approbation of the government and the public expression by the two Houses of the Legislature, at the result of my endeavors to be useful to the Province, I must value most the testimony which the proposed compliment conveys to me from gentlemen whom, independently of every private association of friendship, I cannot but respect the most highly, from their rank and character, and who are exempt by their situations from the influence of those feelings which in public matters, at least, often insensibly bias the judgment. You will do me the justice to believe, that next to the grateful sense I entertain of the honor intended me, is my anxiety to learn that I shall not be thought ungrateful in begging to decline it.

I am, dear sir,

Yours most faithfully and respectfully,

JNO. B. ROBINSON.

REPLY.

York, Oct. 14th, 1823.

J. B. Robinson, Esk., Attorney General:

Dear Sir—I am requested by the gentlemen, who had the honor of waiting upon you on Friday last, to acknowledge your favor of the 11th, and to express their acquiescence in your determination to decline the small proof of private attachment and public respect which they intended. But while they do justice to the delicacy of your motives, they cannot but hope that some other manner of manifesting the high sense they entertain of your services more congenial to your feelings, which have proved so beneficial to the Province and so honorable to its natives.

I remain, dear sir,

Most truly yours,

JAS. BABY.

It cannot be said that he enriched himself at the expense of the country, and I am not aware that any of his sons held positions under the Government in his life time. True, the present Lieutenant-Governor is his next eldest son, and the more to his honor, as being chosen to carry out the views of responsible government and guided by principles no doubt he inherits from his honored and revered father.

Another prominent member of the traduced Family Compact was Chief Justice Sir J. B. McAuley, born at Niagara, 1793, and educated by the late Bishop Strachan. When he joined the Glengarry Fencibles, raised for the special defense of the Upper Province, he received a commission as lieutenant, and afterwards was appointed adjutant in the same corps. At Ogdensburg, Oswego, Lundy's Lane and at the siege at Fort Erie, he was distinguished for his gallantry, never shrinking from the severest conflict and always ready to do his duty no matter where it might lead him. As a laborious and painstaking judge, none exceeded him. We believe there are no two opinions as to the way he discharged the many duties incumbent upon him. His knowledge of the law was extensive, the experience he had gained was great, and ever desirous of rendering justice to the utmost in his power, he laboriously studied everything appertaining to the cases with which he had to deal. Many gentlemen, too, who now stand high in the legal profession, acknowledge with gratitude the assistance they received from him while they were yet students. His motto through life would appear to have been "Whatever thy hand findeth to do, do it with thy whole might. In 1859 the honor of knighthood was conferred upon him by Her Majesty the Queen. He left no sons and a very little property.

In the hurried sketch of these prominent men, I must not omit to mention so many others equally deserving: The McDonalds, Sherwoods, the McLeans, the Hagermans, Boltons, Jones and McNabs. All but the latter were prominent judges, all descendents of U. E. Loyalists and educated by Dr. Strachan, and noted for their unswerving loyalty, honor and integrity, and for the defense of their country, from Christler's farm to Detroit.

The impartial reader in reviewing the services and private worth of these true types of Canadians, will surely and charitably remove the veil which might dim the luster of their deeds, and forget their shortcomings, many as the may have been, and who among our most celebrated states men nowadays, are exempt from them under any government, Liberal or Conservative, and I would fain hope that there are hundreds, nay thousands, in this proud domain, who would cheerfully contribute to the erection of a monument commemorating their deeds, yes, even under the shadow of the immortal Brock, once their companion in arms on the battlefield, and at the council board, and would feel it an honor and pride to trace upon its pedestal Old England's crested motto:

"Honi Soit Qui Mal y Pense."

THE HON. JAMES BABY—OBITUARY NOTICE.

(Taken from Whitby Repository, England.)

It is with extreme concern that we announce to the public the loss of so valuable and respected a member of this Society as the Hon. James Bâby, who, after a very short but severe illness, breathed his last on the afternoon of Tuesday, the 19th of February last, in the 71st year of his age. As very few persons had heard of his illness, the report of his death produced a great sensation, for he was much beloved by all who knew him. His disease was at first attended with excessive pain and repeated convulsions, and when they abated he was reduced to a state of great debility, and had lost the power of articulation. He was nevertheless quite sensible, knew what was said to him, and recognized his friends when they approached him. He seemed fully aware of his approaching dissolution, and bearing his illness with great fortitude and composure, he looked forward to the awful event with tranquil resignation.

Hon. James Bâby, Inspector General.

Those animating hopes with which he had always rested in humble confidence on the mercies of his God enabled him to contemplate death without dismay, and his last moments were marked with that elevated serenity and pious submission which well became the conclusion of a life in which the great duties of a man and a Christian had been conscientiously discharged.

In everything that relates to the life and character of a person so extensively known through both provinces and deservedly beloved, the public will naturally feel a lively curiosity; and we lament that we are unable to meet this laudable desire with any other than a hasty and imperfect sketch of both.   Yet short as our notice must of necessity be, there will be found something to stimulate to moral improvement, something to recommend and inspire the love of virtue, and to exemplify the rewards of rectitude and the consolation of religion.

James Bâby was born at Detroit in 1762. His family was one of the most ancient in the colony, and it was noble. His father had removed from Lower Canada to the neighborhood of Detroit before the conquest of Que-

bec, where, in addition to the cultivation of lands, he was
connected with the fur trade, at that time, and for many
years after, the great staple of the country.   James was
educated at the Roman Catholic Seminary at Quebec,
and returned to the paternal roof soon after the peace
of 1783. The family had ever been distinguished (and
indeed all the higher French families) for their adherence
to the British crown, and to this more than to any other
cause are we to attribute the conduct of the Province of
Quebec during the American war.   Being a great favorite with his father, James was permitted to make an ex-
cursion to Europe before engaging steadily in business;
and after spending some time, principally in England,
he rejoined his family.

Unfortunately the limits assigned by treaty to the
United States embraced within it the larger portion of
his father's property, and the family attachment to the
British government being well known, they were looked
upon with little favor by the American population, and
found it necessary, after much loss and disappointment,
to remove to the south side of the river Detroit, which

constitutes the boundary of Upper Canada. When the Province of Quebec was divided into two distinct governments, Upper and Lower Canada, the subject of this notice became an executive and legislative councillor of the former, and continued in the regular and efficient discharge of the high and important duties of these eminent stations to the day of his death.

Soon after his return from England he became extensively concerned in the fur trade, and other commercial pursuits; but war with the United States having broken out, all business was suddenly and completely stopped by a hostile invasion. Previous to this he had experienced very serious losses in his commercial dealings, and also in the erection of mills on the property still retained within the territories of the United States, and was endeavoring to make such arrangements as would relieve him from all such difficulties, and enable him to attend to his farm and orchard, and to his promising family. The sudden war, and the calamities which it occasioned him, were not the only evils which befell him—about the same time he lost an affectionate wife, leaving five sons and one daughter, all very young.

To this lady, a woman of excellent name, unblemished
worth, and attentive to every conjugal and domestic duty,
he had been married several years, and in her society
had enjoyed the greatest happiness.   Her death gave
him a great shock; nor did he, perhaps, ever wholly recover from the blow, for there were moments when he
felt the loss, even to the last, most deeply, and he never
married again.   The death of Mrs. Bâby appeared to
blast his hopes and derange his purposes, and to throw
him, as it were, adrift on the ocean of life.

The commencement of the war was, perhaps, fortunate for im under his heavy bereavement, for he was immediately called to active service.   He commanded the
militia of the western district, and performed many services highly essential to the preservation of the province.
The people were anxious to win his favor; they had the
most unlimited confidence in his judgment, and at his
request their provisions, their cattle and personal services
were ever ready to support the king's forces in making
head against the enemy.   When it was in contemplation
to withdraw the troops from the western part of the prov-

ince he sent his children to Quebec; and when this event took place, he found his health so much impaired by fatigue and privation, and the grief which still consumed him, that he found it necessary to adopt the advice of his physicians, and to retire to Lower Canada. There he remained with his children till the re-establishment of peace, but not in the enjoyment of health; nor was it till after he had been some time at Sandwich that his strength and energy returned.

His merits had been so conspicuous during the war— his services so disinterested—his losses and privations so great, that government was anxious to confer upon him some mark of approbation; and, knowing that his means had been very much impaired by the sacrifices he had made, it was determined to confer upon him the first of-fice that became vacant, if worthy of his acceptance. As if to meet these views, the office of Inspector General, a place of great responsibility, was in a short time at the dis-posal of government, and was immediately bestowed upon Mr. Baby. The last seventeen years of his life have been spent at York, in the discharge of the duties of his office,

and never has there been the slightest shadow of com-
plaint—a fact the more remarkable as he had to check
every other office in the province, and to pronounce in a
variety of questions, in which numbers were deeply interested; but such was the public confidence in his integrity and honor that not a murmur was ever heard.

As a member of both councils he displayed the most
uncompromising probity; and no influence could induce
him to give up an opinion, which, after mature examina-
tion, he concluded to be right. Owing to his having cultivated both languages, French and English, and sometimes speaking in the one, and sometimes in the other,
he seemed, at times, slow of apprehension; and, after having made up his mind somewhat pertinacious—but it was
the result of high principle—there was nothing of levity
or selfishness allowed in forming his conclusions.

There was a primitive simplicity in Mr. Bâby's character, which, added to his polished manners and benig-
nity of disposition, threw a moral beauty around him that
is very seldom beheld. His favorite amusements partook largely of this simplicity. He was fond of fishing.

The solitude with which it was attended was congenial to his mind—it gave him exercise, fresh air, and an appetite. For this amusement he had always a strong predilection. It required hope and much patience; and, indeed, few can sit quietly on the flowery banks of a calm river, separated from the cares and business of the world, without falling into such contemplations as shall benefit their souls.

He had, perhaps, still greater pleasure in attending to his garden. To prune, to bud and graft, to sow and plant were among his most agreeable employments. He delighted in watching the progress of his labors, and was anxious to discover new methods of improving fruits and plants, and ascertaining the most approved methods of cultivation. He would frequently find him hastening in the morning to enjoy his garden, and no man can be fond of its fruits and flowers, and the delightful enjoyment which they yield both to the eye and ear by their perfumes and colors, without having his heart touched with gratitude to God, their Creator and the giver of all good. This sweet and amiable disposition appeared in all his occupations, and was evident in everything around him. He had a number of canary birds, which he tended with great care, and rejoiced as much in their increase as if he had received some great reward; and when the room resounded with their songs, expressive of their joys, their loves and their happiness, he appeared to participate in their innocent delights. We might proceed to mention the interest which he took in the comfort and happiness of all domestic animals which he kept about him—but we must hasten to a close.

His external accomplishments and manners were highly adapted to win affection's esteem. To an address peculiarly engaging from its dignity, urbanity and ease was united a cordiality and kindness of deportment which induced one to desire a more intimate acquaintance.

In his social intercourse he was a universal favorite for the sweetness of his temper, and innocence of his heart opened the affection of all in his favor. It was not that he was distinguished for his colloquial powers, for he was by no means the leader in conversation, but there was the polish of the most refined manners ripened by innate

benevolence which made him so acceptable in all companies, that those only who have had the happiness of
meeting him often in society can form a just conception
of the pleasure of his presence.

But highly as this excellent man was to be admired
and loved for his engaging manners and virtuous senti-
ments, the exalted qualities which dignified his moral
nature are still more worthy of approbation. These were
the gems which shed around his character that lustre
which made him so great a favorite. A strict probity
and inviolable love of truth were, perhaps, the most
prominent of his moral virtues. From those his conduct derived such a purity and elevation as could only
spring from a mind in which the finest sensibilities of
virtue had ever remained uncontaminated by the con-
sciousness of dishonor. To transmit this precious inher-
itance to his children by precept and example was the
principal study of his life; and to secure to them the per-
manent enjoyment of this valuable deposit he labored un-
ceasingly to inculcate that which he truly deemed the
foundation of every virtue—the principle of religion.

His was not a religion of speculation, but a rule of life which governed all his actions, and not only extended its purifying powers to his intercourse with the world, but it penetrated the retirement of the closest and the secret recesses of the heart. Of christian charities his breast was peculiarly susceptible; he was the friend of the widow, the orphan, and of those who have no helpers, and his regard was powerfully excited by every resemblance to divine goodness, so that to the man possessed of moral worth he was irresistibly drawn as to a brother. But while his benevolence thus extends to all surrounding objects, its flame became more warm and bright to those who were most near; and in the relations of husband, parent and friend, all the kindlier affections of his nature were kindled to their highest fervor.

It was, indeed, his lot to experience many afflicting dispensations in that quarter where his tenderest affections were engaged; but here the consolations of Christian hope and the unshaken assurance of divine goodness were his refuge and support; and while he bowed in resigned submission to that searching discipline with which it was the good pleasure of his God to exercise his faith, he turned with grateful contentment to those blessings which he was yet permitted to enjoy, and which he continued with pious thankfulness and quickened sensibility to cherish and improve to the last moment of his earthly existence.

Thus the severity of his trials proved the stability of his virtue, and his probationary sorrows, by softening his devotion and refining his best disposition, served only to render him better prepared for the felicities of another world. He was a Christian without guile—affable and polished in his manners—courteous in his conversation—dignified in his deportment—warm in his affections—steady in his friendship—and unshaken in his principles. The great object of his life was usefulness, and the spring of all his action was religion. With scarcely a failing to cast a shade over the collective splendor of the estimable endowments which were united in his character and condust, who that knew him can avoid dwelling upon his memory with a sorrowful joy, and feeling that a great blank has been made in our social circle, and that one

of the most worthy of our elders has been gathered to
his fathers.

The funeral took place at eleven o'clock yesterday
morning. It proceeded with all the solemnities of the
Catholic ritual from his late residence to the cemetery
attached to the Catholic church of this town. It was
preceded by about fifty boys in surplice, then the officiat-
ing clergyman, the Very Rev. W. J. O'Grady, B. D. V.
G., accompanied by the venerable the Archdeacon of
York, next the family physicians and then the coffin, supported by the members of the executive council as pall-
bearers. It was the largest and most respectable funeral
we ever witnessed in this country. It was attended by all
the virtue, rank and intelligence of the town and its vicinity, and the countenance of every individual whom we had
an opportunity of observing in that vast assemblage dem-
onstrated the high respect in which Mr. Baby was held.
All business was suspended—every shop and office was
closed—there was no manifestation of sectarian feeling—
the whole community appeared as one common family
united together in bewailing this melancholy bereave-

ment. What an evidence does not this afford, that, however men may rave and look furiously at each other on the minor questions of politics, all can yet agree in paying the tribute of their united respect to incorruptible virtue and integrity. Catholics, Protestants, Presbyterians and Methodists were amalgamated together on this lamentable occasion, and with their respective ministers attended his last obsequies with the greatest decorum and attention. During the funeral sermon, which was preached by the Very Rev. the Vicar General, his auditory appeared powerfully affected. We never before witnessed the ceremonies of the Catholic church on such an occasion performed with greater solemnity; and we sincerely hope that the harmony and union which appeared to pervade all classes of the community may long continue amongst us to heal the divisions of party, to promote Christian charity, to cement us into the nature of one family, and that family into the nature of one heart. —The Canadian Correspondent.

SERVICE ON THE DETROIT FRONTIER DURING THE REBELLION OF '37 AND '38.

It was on or about the 1st of January, 1838, and the hour midnight. I was then living in my log house, two miles above Chatham, keeping bachelor's hall on the banks, "where wandered along the hoary Thames its silver winding way." I was aroused from a profound slumber, induced by a hard day's chopping in the bush, by a tremendous banging at the door, and desiring the intruders to come in, (no bolting of doors in those days), the leather latchet outside, and fastened to the wooden latch within, was violently jerked and three of my boon companions, viz.: James Perrier, Patrick Brereton and V. Sumner entered with a simultaneous exclamation, "We are chilled to the bone, hungry as wolves, and dry as powder horns." So tumbling out of bed I seized the black bottle on the shelf, in the throat of which was thrust a tallow candle, and lighting it threw two or three billets of shag-bark hickory on the smouldering embers,

and in a few moments had a roaring fire, and withdraw-
ing a flagon of rye from underneath my bed, where I
kept it carefully concealed from my negro servant, Andrew Jackson, a bout or two of this soon thawed them
out, and taking from the beam in the adjoining room a
flitch of bacon of my own curing, and shaving some
very fine slices, parboiled for five minutes and frizzled in
a frying pan was a relish fit for an emperor.

In the meantime Jim Perrier had emptied the tin pail
of potatoes that stood in the chimney corner to keep from
freezing, and carefully washing them chucked them into
a pot of boiling water for thirty minutes, and every drop
of water being poured from them, the cover taken off,
and a handful of salt sprinkled over them caused their
jackets to burst and their cheeks to bloom like the rose.
No such bacon, no such potatoes nowadays. The time
is past, and Biddy has lost the art. So sitting around
the board and doing ample justice to the feast, I remarked:

"What's up and what in thunder has brought you
chaps here to knock me up at this hour of the night?"

"Oh, enough, and the devil's to pay," was the rejoinder.
Mackenzie had raised the standard of revolt at Montgomery's tavern, some six or eight miles back of Toronto. Col. McNabb, (afterwards Sir Allan), with his stalwart men of Gore, and the Toronto volunteers, had gone
to the front and dispersed them. Mackenzie had run
the gauntlet and, by a narrow squeak, got to the Niagara frontier, crossed it at Queenston, and a short time
afterwards made Buffalo his headquarters, and Navy
Island, just above the Falls, his field of operations, and
from which he was driven by the capture and destruction of the famed steamer "Caroline," which was set fire
to and sent over the falls in a blaze, several on board,
who could not escape, adding fuel to the flames. Perhaps it would not be out of place here to remark that a
short time previous to these events, Sir Francis Bondhead, the Lieutenant Governor of Upper Canada, had
sent all the troops in his province to aid and assist Sir
John Colborne in Lower Canada to suppress the rebellion there, telling him "he could depend upon the loyalty of the Upper Canadians for defense," and challeng-

ing Mackenzie and his rabble to "come on if they dared."
Rather a hazardous boast, as it proved afterwards.

Whilst Mackenzie was occupying Navy Island his aids
and abettors were busy in other portions of the province.
Doctor (quack) Theller, from Montreal, taking his cue
from Papineau, in Lower Canada, made his appearance
in Detroit, and with the disaffected who ran away with
him, and the offscourings of Detroit, succeeded in rob-
bing the arsenal at Dearborn of some 500 stand of arms,
and two or three pieces of cannon. He made it pretty
lively for the defenceless Canadian frontier and the
surrounding country was called upon to at once
come to their aid. H. J. Jones, J. P. and Crown Land
Agent, had been sent from Chatham to Detroit to see
the authorities there and at Windsor and report the state
of affairs, and on his return gave the above information.
A meeting had been called in the evening at the school
house in Chatham and 100 volunteers enrolled at once.
Capt. Bell, late of the Forty-first or Forty-second Regiment, who fought in Picton's division throughout the
Peninsular war, and was distinguished for his bravery,

having been shot through the jaw and laid on the battlefield of Salamanca during the whole night, (this wound
interfered not a little in giving the word of command in
after years), was chosen captain.   I was chosen first
lieutenant, T. McCrae second, and C. Cartier ensign.

So it was to impart this news to me that I was so un-
ceremoniously disturbed, and I was expected to join the
company at as early an hour as possible the next morning.   It being then 2 a. m. one of them turned in with
me, while the other two laid upon the floor with my buffalo skins and with the backs of chairs turned under for
pillows, slept soundly.   After an early breakfast that
morning I shouldered my double-barrelled gun and we
started for Chatham.   We found the village astir.   James
Read, a merchant, furnished us with a loaf of bread and
two pounds of pork each and acted as commissary.   He
engaged ten or twelve teams to take us to Dauphin's,
twelve miles from Chatham, down the river a little below
which commenced the Raleigh and Tilbury plains, covered with two or three feet of water and two inches thick
of ice, through which the teams could not pass, so they

dumped us there and returned home. With great difficulty and hardship breaking through the ice, we got to
the lighthouse some six miles distant, where we struck
dry land. We reached Stony Point that evening and
bivouacked among the farmers. The shrill clarion of
chanticleer awoke us the next morning and we proceeded
on our way to Brooker and Shaver's inns, about twelve
miles from Windsor on Lake St. Clair, a little below
which we encountered another marsh, suffering the same
hardships as through the Tilbury marsh or plains. As
we approached the ferry we were met by some of the
Windsor inhabitants, prominent among whom was my
friend and kinsman, James Dougall, who gave us a kind
reception and was unremitting in his attention to our
eveiy want, providing us with comfortable quarters and
serving out to each of us the next day a new four-point
blanket, which proved our greatest comfort.

On the night following, which, I think, was on the
7th of January, the steam ferry "United," Capt. Clinton,
(father of the present manager of the ferry company), in
command, was ordered to hold herself in readiness to take

us down to Amherstburg, as "General" Theller, so-called, threatened an invasion there that night. About 9 p. m. we, that is, forty men of Major Ambridge's company, forty of the Kent volunteers (of which I was put in command), and twenty of the Windsor company under Capt. W. G. Hall, in all one hundred men, with Col. Radcliff in command, proceeded down the river, the thermometer at zero. On nearing Fighting Island we met the steamer "General Brady" on her way up from Bois Blanc Island under the control of Tom Mason, as he was familiarly called, the Governor of Michigan, who, at the request of the authorities on both sides of the river, had gone down that morning with the avowed intention of dispersing the so-called patriots, but it was afterwards creditably reported that he indulged in several bottles of champagne in his cabin upon the trip and knew no more of what was going on on board ship than if he had been in Turkey. As we approached and were passing this steamer, to our great surprise, several shots were fired at us, but fortunately no one was hit.

Proceeding on our way to Amherstburg we reached the Lime Kiln crossing and, it being moonlight, we discovered the schooner "Ann" moored in front of the old barracks and now and then discharging her cannon upon the defenseless town. On discovering this, Col. Radcliff ordered an immediate landing at the Lime Kilns and we quartered ourselves as best we could in the Huron Indian huts, they being the only inhabitants along the river front at that time. Towards daylight an order came from headquarters, viz., Col. Prince, Maj. Laughlin, and Col. Radcliff, for us to proceed to Amherstburg and receive orders as to our movements. On arriving there the company halted and I proceeded to the house of the late James Gorden, where the above named officials were quartered, and finding Col. Prince, he cheerfully accompanied me to Bullock's tavern and, kicking open the door, the house being unoccupied, desired me to take possession and help ourselves to what we chose and to render a strict account of everything used. We soon regaled ourselves with what it contained in viands and wines, and about 9 a. m. received orders to march to Elliot's point, where we took up our quarters in the old Elliot house, as also did Capt. W. G. Hall with his twenty men.

About 7 p. m. on the 9th of January, 1838, the wind being fresh from the northwest and bright moonlight, the schooner "Ann" was discovered leaving her moorings and coming down the river with all sails set, followed by a number of persons along shore peppering away at her with shot guns, rifles, pistols, etc., and as she approached the point, (Elliott's), through floating ice, a galling fire was opened upon her from behind the large trees on the point, and immediately she grounded, affording a splendid target for our sharpshooters, who made it lively for the crew on board.

Col. Radcliffe had followed her down with the crowd, and on his arrival opposite and close to the vessel, called for volunteers to board her. I soon found myself with others struggling in the ice to accomplish this, and on reaching the vessel one got on the back of the other, who in turn assisted others, until some twenty or thirty got on board. H. Leighton and two or three others were on board before us. All appeared as still as the grave.

Gen. Anderson laid alongside the bulwarks shot through
the chest, and died that morning in our quarters, in the
old Elliott house.   Col. Dodge, a Toledo lawyer, was
found with his right eye hanging on his cheek, caused
by a spent ball. Capt. Brophy was also wounded, and
found near the cabin door, also one Davis.   On inquiring for the rest of the crew we were told that "General"
Theller was in the hold of the vessel with some twenty
or thirty others, and had closed the hatches over them.
On the hatches being removed I called for Theller to surrender, which he did by standing up and handing me his
sword, and claiming my protection.   No doubt he was
terrified at our appearance, and with our blankets
wrapped around our shoulders, probably took us for
Mohawk Indians.   He was bareheaded and in his stocking feet, and wore a military frock coat, with a gilt star
on his left breast. Extending him my hand I drew him
up on deck and the others soon followed.   I then ordered them to jump overboard and they would find many
on shore to receive them.   Theller said he was exhausted
and bruised from the recoil of his cannon, so jumping

into the water and ice he managed to get on my back and I carried him ashore, on reaching which our clothes immediately froze stiff, and it was with difficulty we reached our quarters, some hundred and fifty yards or more.

Towards morning (three or four o'clock I should say) Col. Prince entered our quarters, where he found us toasting before an open fireplace, and inquired for "General" Theller, who was lying on the floor in the corner of the room, with my blanket for a covering, and a billet of wood for a pillow. Pointing him out to the colonel the latter, in the most unceremonious manner, awoke him by a kick in the ribs. To my dying day I shall never forget that ludicrous scene. Theller sitting on his haunches and beholding the colonel for the first time in his life. If Tecumseh, Pontiac or Black Hawk had risen from their graves and appeared before him they could not have inspired more terror in his mind. A red fox-skin bonnet, rather than cap, covered his head; a doe-skin jacket encircled his burly shoulders and loins, tied by a red sash, in which was thrust a pair of horse pistols and a kind of cutlass; corduroy breeches and leather gaiters reaching to the top of his English heavily spiked laced boots finished his toilet distingue. Addressing Theller, after the kick, the colonel said:

"Get up, you d—d piratical scoundrel."

Theller appealing to me said: "Captain Bâby, I surrendered myself a prisoner to you, and now I claim your protection."

To which I replied: "The colonel is my superior officer and I have nothing to say."

"Let me have my boots and cap, then," said Theller.

"You won't want either before daylight," was the colonel's rejoinder.

"Bâby," continued the colonel, "see that a rope be provided, to which securely fasten all the prisoners two abreast and then tie the same to the end of a cart (which had hastily been provided) so that they can be safely conveyed to the guard house at Amherstburg," which was done accordingly. Theller, Dodge and Brophy were unable to walk and were bundled into the cart, to the end of which the rope was tied, and away it went with its kite-tail of prisoners to the guard

house, upon which being reached it was decided, by the
authorities, to send the prisoners at once to London by the
lake shore route, to avoid the danger of a rescue, if sent by
the frontier. They all reached London safely under a strong
guard of volunteers, twenty of whom belonged to my company.

Colonel Prince's treatment of Theller would appear to be
harsh, cruel, and unofficer-like, but when it is considered
that the inhabitants along the whole frontier, and he and his
family in particular, were in a constant state of fear and
trembling, expecting that every moment their houses would
be fired and they murdered by these piratical ruffians (which
they did the year following at the Battle of Windsor), Prince
well knew the characters he had to deal with and he treated
them as they well deserved.

Theller, Brophy and Dodge were sent to the citadel at
Quebec, to be there securely held for further disposal, but
from which, by some unaccountable means, the former and
the latter escaped and reached the American shore, and
some years after, Theller published a book of his adventures.
The other prisoners, some twenty-six in number, were tried

in London; half of them were hanged there, and the other half transportd for a certain number of years, and returned to the country after the time had expired.

A short time after the cart aforesaid and its kite-tail of prisoners had vanished in the distance, I received orders to return, at once, with the remainder of my company to Windsor, as another invasion was expected there at night, which, on our arrival, proved a false alarm.

Nothing particular occurred along the frontier until in the month of February (I forget the exact date) an invasion of the so-called patriots was made on Fighting Island, about six miles below Detroit, and we, the Kent volunteers, with others were ordered to the front. We left Windsor at 4 a. m. The snow was a foot deep. We arrived at a farmer's (Gignac's, I think) barn along the road, which was situated immediately opposite the island, and to our agreeable surprise found Major Townsend with a detachment of the 32d Regiment from Amherstburg resting in lee of it from the piercing cold northerly wind. Ascertaining who we were he gave us a warm reception, remarking, "We'll have some fun before breakfast." He was only waiting for daylight to see his way. In the meantime, Captain Glascow, with three pieces of artillery, had taken up a position commanding a fair sweep of the island, which was covered with a thick growth of burr oaks with their dried leaves still upon them. He opened a fire of grape shot upon the invaders, who were sitting around their camp fires, and such was the effect that before we had time to cross over to the island, not a soul was to be seen. They recrossed the river on the ice, which was a foot and a half thick, and were received with open arms by hundreds of persons on the American shore, in sleighs, who were waiting to hear the result of the fight. The only trophy was a small six-pounder captured by the Kent volunteers, which we took to Chatham, when we were disbanded and relieved by the 2nd Battalion towards the end of April. Thus ended my four month's service as a volunteer.

In reviewing the events of the Rebellion of 1837 and 1838 to-day, the fact is established that by its suppression this Canada of ours has been preserved to the British Crown, its brightest gem, all praise to the descendants of the U. E. Loyalists—those hearts of oak—the Corinthian pillars of

Canada to-day. All honor to those of the Old Family Compact; and glory to the brave and gallant volunteers, who belonged to neither, but put their shoulders to the wheel and accomplished it.

As already stated we were relieved by the Second Battalion in April, and being composed principally of farmers and mechanics returned home. December 4th, 1839, the battle of Windsor took place.

The following account of the capture of the schooner Ann is taken verbatim from Theller's "Canada," 1837-1838, pages 136 and 137.

"As we neared the town volley after volley was poured into us with considerable effect, and with more skill than the night before. It was no boys' play now, many of our men were wounded and considerable damage to the rigging. Captain Davis, who was holding on to the anchor, was shot in the wrist, and from which he afterwards died, and away went the anchor. The enemy aimed with fatal precision at the helmsman, and he fled below, leaving the boat to her own will, and as the down-hauls had been cut away by the shot the sails could not be managed. Unskilled as mariners, confusion reigned among us, and the schooner drifting with the ice, we were in a few moments aground on the main shore, our deck presenting an inclined front to the irritated and triumphant marksmen of the enemy. Dodge, Brophy, myself and a few others, determined to sell our lives at as dear a rate as possible, and still hoping that the force on the island would come to our rescue, maintained for a while our position on the deck, and with much labor brought our cannon to bear upon the shore. Another volley and a rush to board us. The moon was shining bright, and we were easily seen and marked by their riflemen, while they were concealed behind the fences and the trees of an orchard close at hand. Dodge was wounded in the eye, and fell, as I then thought, dead at my feet; Brophy was soon after disabled by a wound. A little boy, a Canadian refugee engaged in bringing us loaded muskets, was killed in the act, fell overboard, and his body found on shore the next morning. All around me were soon disabled. The little time I had to think disclosed my probable fate in case of surrender. No other alternative seemed left but a preferable death on the spot, and in the act of discharging the gun myself, I received a blow on the head that felled me to the deck and down the hatchway to the hold. Stunned and senseless, I was dragged out by the victors, and placed in custody for future disposition. On recovering, I found myself and others in the charge of Lieut. Bâby (the author), who protected me from insult, and who was aided in this manly duty by Captain Rudyard and Colonel Radcliff, the latter saying in my hearing that we were prisoners of war, had conducted ourselves like brave men, and must not be abused, but be handed over to the proper authorities for judicial treatment. I was taken to the hospital (the old Elliott Homestead, our barracks pro tem., then unoccupied by W. L. Bâby), to which had been previously carried Dodge, Brophy, Davis, Anderson, Smith and Thayer, all seriously wounded."

VISIT OF THE PRINCE OF WALES TO DETROIT IN SEPTEMBER, 1860.

——

August 15, 1812.—On the eve of that eventful day four individuals left the hamlet of Sandwich, and ascended the river for two miles. This brought them to the ground on which the present building of the S. & W. street car and express office now stands. The primeval forest nearly clothed the abrupt and craggy bank along the silent stream, save the clumps and scattered Normandy pear trees that struggled through the native oaks and elms, filled with their luscious fruit. The air is still and periodically broken by the hoarse and mournful sound of the bullfrogs heard for miles below, commencing with a single note and swelling into a grand chorus of 10,000. Arriving at this spot, the trees that had encumbered it had been removed the day previous, and a space to work a park of five pieces of artillery made under the able supervision of Capt. Dixon, Royal Artillery. Of the four individuals forming this group, one demands our first attention. About six feet in height, his well-shaped feet incased in a pair of highly polished Wellington boots, coming well up and over the knee; his well-fitting doe skin breeches, the scarlet uniform of a commanding officer wraps with admirable fit his well-developed chest, displaying to advantage his many clasps and medals, a black cocked hat surmounted by three white ostrich plumes, which drooped and shaded his beaming, though determined and brave countenance. This is the intrepid Gen. Brock.

The one at his elbow commands our next attention. He is not quite so tall, but equally well built. Wellington boots up to the knee he would discard. His path leads him over the moss-covered, prostrate oak, to trace with stealthy step the snow-tracked timid deer, to spring and light with tender foot in his birch bark frail canoe, and trap the wary beaver in his work of toil. Moccasins of elk or deer skin, adorned with colored quills of porcupine, displaying his well-formed feet; leggings of the same material, the seams cut with deep fringe, a leather jacket trimmed the same, a light silk shawl with tuft of eagle feathers shades his nut-brown face, and thus stood the forest king, Tecumseh. The two others (McKee, the Indian agent and interpreter, and Col. Elliott, brothers in arms of Tecumseh), formed the group. When ready to return to their quarters, Brock called to his side Dixon, and thus instructed him, "You will open your battery at sunrise to-morrow. Yonder lies the Fort (Shelby)," pointing with his finger to the spot where now stands the new postoffice, "and to-morrow morning at nine we will attempt the capture of the fort." On the following morning the attack was made, and the fort surrendered without the loss of a single man on the part of the British and two or three killed and wounded in the fort only.

The fort having surrendered, Brock found himself possessor of 2,000 prisoners, 24,000 stands of arms, 43 pieces of artillery, 100,000 cartridges, 40 barrels of powder and a large supply of provisions.* On the 17th Brock recrossed the river with Tecumsch, Split Log (Tecumseh's brother-in-law) and other celebrated Indian chiefs, with François Bâby, uncle to the author, the relator, in the same boat, when it was observed that Brock appeared lost in profound meditation, and, suddenly recovering himself, he gently placed his hand on the shoulder of

*See Farmer's History of Detroit.

Tecumseh and said (to McKee, the Indian interpreter), "Tell this brave man that this will prove a proud day for England, and to him in a great measure belongs the greater honor, and, as proof of my admiration and esteem, ask him if he will accept of this gift?" at the same time presenting him with his pair of silver mounted pistols. The dusky warrior eyed him with a soft and tender smile, and the confidence of an eastern prince, gracefully declined, and, pointing his finger at Split Log, said: "The services of my brother chief are equal to mine, and I cannot wound his feelings by appearing thus his superior."

Brock, perceiving at once the motive that actuated this truly brave man, made ample amends by presenting, himself, the weapons to Split Log, and, unwinding his sash from his waist, asked him (Tecumseh) to accept of it, which he cheerfully did, and tradition relates that this sash was found encircling his loins when his body was found on the battlefield of Moravian Town.

September 20, 1860—Forty years gone by, and let us recall to mind the scene of that day in 1812. We are standing on that same spot where Capt. Dixon, of the Royal Artillery, opened his battery of five guns on the Fort (Shelby). Let us figure to our minds the four individuals mentioned in that group—Brock, Tecumseh, McKee and Elliott. The face of nature is changed. The banks of the beautiful river adorned with huge blocks of houses of commerce and hotels, the wharves are encumbered with steamers of our inland seas, from their utmost limits; the mansions, villas and private residences of its industrious inhabitants crowd every available lot on land and stream. All is bustle, strife and energy. A sound fills the earth that thrills the air with joy and gladness. Our gracious Queen has sent the pride of her throne to visit her loyal and true sons of her far distant realm. The white and frosty-haired old veteran, who fought her battles north, east, south and west in long passed years and has chosen his quiet and peaceful home in the forest-encumbered wilderness, ncovers his head and mentally exclaims, "God save the Queen." All classes of people vie with each other in paying him the greatest honor. The French clergy in pontificial robes receive him with homage; the English clergy meet him with open arms and exult in paying him that profound respect and

veneration as the son of their noble Queen; the red and
swarthy children of the forest are anxious to extend the
hand of friendship and bid him welcome; the sons of Africa,
freed from the chains of slavery that once oppressed them,
and now as free as the air they breathe, wish him "God-
speed."

At 6 p. m. on the 27th of September an anxious crowd
are waiting for his appearance at the Great Western Depot
in Windsor. Clergymen, mayors, sheriffs, wardens, reeves
and councilors, etc., choke the entrance. The train arrives,
and the prince, with his staff, steps on board the steamer
(ferryboat) Windsor, Capt. W. R. Clinton in command.
The staff consists of his grace, the Duke of Newcastle, the
Earl of St. Germain, Gen. F. Williams, Maj.-Gen. Bruce,
Lord Lyons, Maj. Tresdale, Capt. Gray, Dr. Aikland, etc.
So great is the jam that it is impossible for the prince to
reply to the different addresses of the people. But he did
so in time. Some people had an idea that the prince would
appear in gorgeous gold and purpled robe, with crown of
spangled jewels; and yet how amazed and astonished when,
stepping forth to receive their homage, they beheld the son

of Victoria. A boy 19 years of age, about 5 feet 8 inches, rather slim, a white silk hat held in his mauve gloved right hand, in his left a slender cane; light, grey-colored suit of admirable fit encased his well-formed, royal, youthful and princely body and limbs; light brown hair wafted to the right side exposed his white forehead; soft, beaming blue eyes, an aquiline nose, with pouting lips and cheeks with a bloom of a maiden of 16; such appeared Albert Edward. A dusky gloom proclaims a sombre night. As the steamer (Windsor) approaches the centre of the river, she is intercepted and surrounded by a fleet of steamers, tugs and yachts that choke the stream a half a mile wide. The sky is illuminated with designs and mottoes on flag and pennon and sides of steamers. On one directly in front, in transparent light, is, "Nemo me impune lacessit;" on another, "The rough burr-thistle spreading wide amang the bearded beer, I turned my weeding clips aside an spar'd the symbol dear." Again, "Briton's sons welcome Baron Renfrew to the land of their adoption;" "Welcome, laddie, for yer mither's sake." One blaze of reflecting light springs from the side of a barge anchored in midstream, and displays the coat of arms of Great Britain, again the goddess of liberty, and then the queen and Washington, and from the roofs of houses and decks of steamers the heavens are ablaze with brilliant rockets and Roman candles. At last the steamer arrived at the foot of Woodward avenue, where 100,000 spectators awaited him, and, amid cheers and waving of handkerchiefs and the sound of the national airs, he is conveyed to his quarters.

The forest chief Tecumseh and the plumed warrior Brock are still spectators of this scene (we will imagine), when the chief remarks, "My friend, what means this vast and gorgeous display?" And Brock replies, "They are paying homage to the heir of that mighty throne for which you and I fought and bled forty-eight years gone by." "It would appear they are fast friends now," remarks the chief. "And why not?" replies the warrior. "Are they not all of one family, in descent, in blood, in language, in habits and customs?" The sword should never be drawn to end their disputes. Let us hope that wisdom will ever prevail, to avert it, and by firmly extending the hand of friendship they may live on in brotherly love, so say we all.

How highly amused must the prince have been on perusing the following article the next morning:

Artemus Ward, the showman, the man of many experiences and unlimited humor, has seen the prince.

The interview between these distinguished persons is supposed to have taken place at Sarnia, and A. Ward, Esq., tells the story as follows:

He handed me a segar, and we sot down on the pizarro and commensed smokin' rite cheerful. "Wall," saz I, "Albert Edard, how's the old folks?" "Her majesty and the prince are well," he sed. "Duz the old man take his lager reglar?" I inquired. The prince larfed and intermated that the old man didn't let many kegs of that bevridge spile in the sellar in the coarse of a yere. We sot and tawked there sum time abowt matters and things, and bimeby I axed him how he liked bein' prince as fur as he'd got. "To speak plain, Mr. Ward," he sed, "I don't much like it. I'm sick of all this bowin' and scrapin' and crawlin' and hurrain' over a boy like me. I wood rather go threw the country quietly and enjoy myself in my own way, with other boys, and not be made a show of to be garped at by everybody.

When the people cheer me, I feel pleased, fur I know thay
meen it, but if these one-hoss offishuls cood know how I see
threw all their movements and understand exackly what
they air after, and know'd how I larf at 'em in private, thay'd
stop kissin' and fawnin' over me as they do.   But you know,
Mr. Ward, I can't help being a prince, and I must do all I
kin to fit myself for the persishun I must some time ockepy."
"That's troo," sez I.   "Sickness and the doctors will carry
the queen orf one of these dase, sure's yer born."   The time
having arove fur me to take my departer, I rose up and sed:
"Albert Edard, I must go, but previs to doin' so I will observe that you soot me.   Yu're a good feller, Albert Edard,
and tho' I'm agin princes as a gineral thing, I must say I
like the cut of yure gib.   When you git to be king, try and
be as good a man as yure mither has bin.   Be just and jen-
erus, espeshully to showmen, who have allers bin aboozed
sins the dase of Noah, who was the fust man to go into the
menagery bizness, and ef the daily papers of his time air to
be beleeved, Noah's colleckshun of living wild beests beet
ennything ever seen sins, tho' I make bowld to dowt ef his
snaiks was ahead of mine.   Albert Edard, adoo."   I tuk his

hand, which he shook warmly, and givin' him a perpetooal free pars to my show and also parses to take home for the queen and old Albert, I put my hat on and walkt away. "Mrs. Ward," I solilerquized as I walkt along, "Mrs. Ward, ef you cood see yure husband now, as he prowdly emirjis from the presents of the futur king of England, you'd be sorry you kalled him a beest jest becawz he cum home tired one nite and wanted to go to bed without takin' orf his boots. Yu'd be sorry for trying to deprive yure husband of the priceless boon of liberty, Betsy Jane."

COL. JOHN PRINCE.

THE BATTLE OF WINDSOR, FOUGHT DEC. 4,
1839.

The Report of the Battle taken from an Original Document,
Used in the Trial of Col. Prince.

The following narrative of facts connected with the action
of the 4th of December, is furnished by eye-witnesses and
actors in that affair. It has been withheld to this date, that
time might be allowed for excitement to subside, and opportunity afforded the authors of any erroneous or hasty statements, given officially, or otherwise, to make the necessary
corrections. But the time has arrived when it would be
highly culpable longer to withhold its publication. Several
weeks have elapsed since the appearance of two statements
of the affair, both extremely deficient and erroneous in many
important points, and greatly calculated, whether inten-
tionally or not, to mislead the public. As no corrections of
these statements have been made, either by their authors or
others, a longer silence would tend to sanction and per-
petuate the misconceptions they have but too generally pro-

duced. The contributors to this narrative think it due to the public, and to themselves, that there should be no misconceptions in an affair of so much importance—that "even-handed justice" should be meted out to all concerned. They, therefore, uninfluenced by partialities or prejudices, and solely for the cause of truth, submit their statement to the public, pledging themselves for its correctness in all its essential points, and holding themselves ready to substantiate what they thus set forth.

To give a correct view of the affair, it is necessary to commence the narrative with a brief outline of the circumstances some weeks antecedent to the day of the attack.

From about the first of November it was reported, and generally believed, that large bodies of brigands, from all parts of the United States, were wending their way to the State of Michigan for the purpose of invading our country. The point of attack was variously stated to be Malden, Sandwich, and Windsor. The inhabitants of the two latter places were kept in a constant state of excitement and alarm by their proximity to Detroit, the reputed headquarters of the enemy, and the want of sufficient means to repel any serious invasion. To add to their anxiety and alarm, Major Reid, of the 32d Regulars, who held the command at Sandwich, was called to the London District, and that important trust devolved on Col. John Prince. The effective force at that time consisted of Company No. 1, and 11 men of Company No. 2, Provincial Volunteer Militia, commanded by Capt. Sparke, and four companies of Col. Prince's battalion, commanded respectively by Captains Fox, Lewis, Thebo and Elliott. To Captain Lewis was committed the charge of the important post at Windsor.

With so small a force it was necessary to maintain the greatest watchfulness against any sudden attack; and to ensure that vigilance so essential to our safety, nearly all the inhabitants of Sandwich, not connected with any of the above companies, acted as voluntary night patrol. As more definite and certain information of the strength and intentions of the brigands was received, our situation became the more alarming. Some of our most respectable and influential inhabitants waited on Colonel Prince with a request that he would ask Col. Airey, commanding at Mal-

den, to send up one or two companies of Regulars. Their
request Col. Prince declined complying with, intimating
something like a fear that such an application would be considered as an evidence of cowardice—assuring the gentleman that his battalion was abundantly able to protect them
from any attack of the enemy. His assurances, however,
had little weight in allaying the alarm of the public; nor was
it lessened by the painful discovery that the post at Windsor
had been entrusted to an officer utterly unqualified for such
an important station. Night after night was Capt. Lewis
detected by the Volunteer Patrolle in the most culpable neg-
ligence. His sentinels were placed without judgment, and
their duties were performed in the most slovenly and un-
soldier-like manner. Indeed, it became too apparent to
every reflecting observer, that the post was liable and likely
to be surprised whenever the enemy might think proper to
make the experiment. Under such circumstances, Francis
Bâby, Robert Mercer and James Dougall, Esquires, addressed a request to Col. Airey that a part of Capt. Bell's
Company (No. 2 Provincial Volunteers), then doing duty as
sentinels at Malden, might be sent to Windsor, and Capt.

Lewis' Company be called to Malden to take their place.
This request, most unfortunately, as the sequel proves, was
not granted.

On Friday, the 30th of November, information was received from unquestionable authority, that a large body of
brigands, say from 400 to 600, were assembled on the farms
of Mr. Marrantete and Major Forsyth, about two miles
below the city of Detroit. Their watch-fires on that evening were distinctly seen from Sandwich, and stimulated the
Volunteer Patrolles to double vigilance. On Saturday, the
1st of December, intelligence was brought that early on that
morning the greater part of them had left their camp and
spread themselves among the lower order of taverns in
Detroit, making "Uncle Ben Woodworth's" their headquarters. It was said that a considerable body had also
passed the city and encamped in the vicinity of the "Poor
House," on the Fort Gratiot road, about two miles out of
town. On Sunday, the 2d, it was known that the encampment on the farm of Mr. Marrantete had been visited by a
detachment of United States troops, headed by Gen. Brady
and Major Payne, who put to flight the few brigands who

were left there as a guard, and captured thirteen boxes of arms. A report was current on that day that one of their leaders, and a "sub-treasurer" of their military chest, had absconded, and with all the funds. On Monday, the 5th, it was stated, and generally believed, that disheartened by the foregoing misfortunes, the brigands had abandoned their undertaking and dispersed. Certain it is, that very few of the ruffians were to be seen on that day in Detroit, and "Uncle Ben's" was as deserted as it generally is, or as any other establishment of the kind could be which had been made the rendezvous of such polluting scoundrels. Deceived by these appearances, and trusting to the known and untiring vigilance of Gen. Brady, and above all, relying on what was believed the impassable state of the river, the Volunteer Patrolle, unfortunately, on that night relaxed its usual vigilance, leaving the safety of all our inhabitants, and all that was dear to them, to the keeping of Capt. Lewis. Most unfortunately Gen. Brady, too, deceived by the same circumstances, and depending on Judge McDonnell, Collector, to have the steamer Champlain (the only boat not laid up, or in the employ of the United States) rendered useless by the removal of her valves, relaxed also in his accustomed vigilance. Judge McDonnell did not discharge the trust reposed in him—and our watchful foes, possessed of all these circumstances, took advantage of them, and at one o'clock on the morning of Tuesday, the 4th, about 240 of them seized the Champlain. We do not learn that there was any resistance on the part of her crew—certainly there could have been none worth mentioning, or the alarm would have reached Gen. Brady. After raising steam, the boat was cast off and landed our invaders at 3 o'clock a. m. on the farm of Alexis Pelette, about four miles above the village of Windsor, which latter place is directly opposite the city of Detroit, the Capital of the State of Michigan, and two miles above the town of Sandwich.

It is here to be observed, that although so many on both sides of the river were lulled into fancied security by the acts of the brigands, yet, all were not so deceived. Several loyal subjects residing in Detroit had ferreted out their deep laid plans. Three of these truly "patriotic" fellows having obtained certain intelligence that an attack would be made on Monday night, came over late on the afternoon of that day and gave information at the Barracks to that effect. One of the three enrolled the same evening in Capt. Lewis' Company; another, his companion, remained with him in the Barracks; and the third, knowing his doom should the brigands prove successful, proceeded to Malden. The two former fell martyrs to loyalty and love of country, while gallantly defending the Barracks.

From Pelette's farm the brigands marched down to Windsor without being challenged or opposed. When they had nearly arrived at the Barracks, occupied by a part of Capt. Lewis' company, two of their number, who had been sent in advance to reconnoitre, were met and challenged by the Cavalry Patrolle. As they did not answer the challenge, the Patrolle turned and rode back to the Barracks, and relating the circumstance to the sentinel proceeded to report to Capt. Lewis, whose quarters were about one-quarter of a mile further down the road. As soon as the two men had approached within sight of the sentinel he challenged, and receiving no answer, levelled his piece to fire, the enemy simultaneously doing the same. By a singular coincidence the pieces of both parties missed fire. The sentinel stepped inside the Barracks to reprime and give the alarm. When he stepped out again he found the head of a column of brigands had reached the point where he had first seen the two men. He fired his piece at this body, and again entered the Barracks to rouse its inmates to action. The few men on duty promptly answered the call by rushing out and opening a galling fire upon the advancing foe; killing one of their captains, named Lewis, and wounding several of their men. The brave sentinel (Otterbury), forcing his way through his companions to have another shot and holding up his musket to facilitate his movements, received a ball and two buckshot in his left arm, which obliged him to retire from the conflict. As long as their ammunition held out, our men made a most gallant resistance; and when it failed, ten or twelve effected their retreat, and the rest about 113, surrendered to the enemy, who set fire to the Barracks and the adjoining house belonging to Mr. Francois Jannette, which, with the house occupied by Mr. Retter, were burned to the ground. An inoffensive colored man, named Mills, who resided near the scene of action, coming out of his house to see what was the matter, was taken by the brigands, and on refusing to join them was barbarously shot. From the Barracks the brigands proceeded to set on fire the steamboat Thames, belonging to Duncan McGregor, Esq., and then laid up at Mr. Van Allen's wharf, nearly opposite. They did not succeed in their first attempt, but in an hour afterwards accomplished their purpose. When the boat was fired they compelled Mr. Black and others of our people to assist them in getting her yawl out of the ice, in which they placed some of their party who had been wounded in the attack on the Barracks, and sent them over to Detroit.

From Captain Lewis' quarters the horse patrol proceeded to give the alarm at Sandwich. In a very short time Captain Sparke with No. 1 and about eight men of No. 2 companies of Provincial Volunteer Militia (amounting in the whole to not more than 40 men) together with a number of the inhabitants of the town, were on the march for Windsor. They were immediately followed and overtaken before arriving at the scene of action, by about 60 men of Col. Prince's Battalion of Essex Militia, under the command of Fox, Thebo, and Elliott. On their way up, they were met by various persons retreating from Windsor, among whom was Capt. Lewis, who stated that his Barracks had been attacked and fired, and his men defeated; but with what loss he could not tell, as he had immediately left the place.

When the entire party had arrived at Mr. Maillioux, about half a mile below Windsor, Capt. Thebo, with his company left the road and made a detour so as to come in the rear of the village, a maneuvre, which in the sequel proved of great advantage, as enabling our brave militia to cut off many of the brigands in their subsequent flight towards the woods. The other parties continued their march up the road and at a short distance below the entrance of the village, Captain Sparke halted and formed his men—while the militia under Captains Fox and Elliott, also halted and were marshaled by Capt. Bell, of the 2nd Company, Provincial Volunteers, assisted by Capt. Leslie, of Col. Prince's Battalion. Both parties then resumed the march, and when arrived at the lower end of the village, again halted to reconnoitre. Intelligence was quickly brought by James Dougall, Chas. Bâby and W. R. Wood,

Esquires, who had gone some distance in advance, that the enemy (about 130 in number) had been drawn up across the road, but were then filing to the left into an orchard belonging to Francois Bâby, Esq. Instantly the militia led by Capt. Bell struck off the road into the orchard of Mr. Jannette, and marching up along the fence opened a well-directed fire upon the enemy. In the meantime Captain Sparke with his command and the volunteer inhabitants, who had joined him, continued his march directly up the road, and on arriving at the spot where the enemy had left it, discovered them ensconced in the orchard and in the act of returning the fire which had been opened upon them by Captains Fox and Elliott. Captain Sparke wheeled his command off the road and after pouring a well directed fire, led his gallant followers over an intervening fence to give the brigands the steel. But the rascals waited not the touch of British bayonets—returning the fire, they "broke cover" and fled across the fields in the direction of the woods. Pursuit was given by the whole party and continued to the edge of the woods, by Captains Fox and Elliott, preceded by Capt. Thebo, whose judicious position brought him well to the left of the enemy. Several of the brigands were killed in the chase, among whom were their leaders, Putnam and Harvell, the "Big Kentuckian"; and one of their standard bearers (whose colors were captured by Ensign Rankin, of Captain Sparke's company) and a great number were wounded. Many of them, to expedite their flight, relieved themselves of their arms, accoutrements, and ammunition, and even of parts of their clothing. One man of Capt. Elliott's company was killed, and another wounded in this short but brilliant affair. Captain Sparke finding the pursuit in excellent hands, halted his party when about half a mile from the main road, preparatory to marching back to dislodge any party who might have remained in Windsor. Just at this time Col. Prince made his first appearance on the field, though some think he may have arrived a few moments sooner, as being dressed in a fustian shooting coat and fur cap, he might not have been immediately recognized. However that may be, at this important moment he informed Captain Sparke and the other officers of the party that he had just received intelligence that upwards of two hundred brigands were marching down from Detroit

on the American side for the purpose of crossing over
and attacking Sandwich in front, and that another body
had gone round through the groves to attack it in the
rear. From this statement of Col. Prince, it was deemed
advisable to retire to Sandwich without delay, in order to
defend that place, where all our ammunition, provisions and
the only guns we possessed were deposited. The men who
were in triumphant pursuit of the flying foe were immediately recalled, and Col. Prince ordered the whole force to
march back to Sandwich at double quick time. Before the
party left the field Adjutant Cheeseman, of the 2nd Essex,
who had acted as a volunteer, brought up a prisoner whom
he had taken. He surrendered him to Col. Prince, who
ordered him to be shot upon the spot, and it was done accordingly. Previous to the commencement of our retro-
grade movement, and during its progress, several persons
joined us, bringing various accounts of the strength of a
rear guard or reserve of the brigands which was still in
possession of Windsor. This body, headed (as is said) by
General Birse, at the time the action commenced in the
orchard, was drawn up in front of the burning barracks.

It afterwards advanced nearly opposite the place where Captain Sparke had crossed the fence. Just at this time, Mr. Morse, Commissary, and Doctor Hume, of the medical staff, and others came from Sandwich in a wagon, and drove directly up to it, thinking it was a party of our own militia. As Mr. Morse jumped out of the wagon in front, and was about to address them he was stopped by a young woman, who informed him of their true character. Mr. Morse quickly communicated the intelligence to Doctor Hume and retreated round the corner of an adjoining house. As the doctor attempted to retreat, holding a pistol in his hand, and keeping his "face to the foe," the brigands presented their pieces at him. Mr. Tyas Baker, who had also approached the party, believing them to be friends, called out, "do not shoot that man, he is the doctor," and seeing one of their pieces flash, in the attempt to kill him, again called out, "do not shoot that man, he is our doctor." The brigands turned towards Tyas and demanded, "then why does he not surrender?" This pause caused by the enquiry, enabled the doctor to get past the corner of a house, under cover of which he crossed a fence and gained the rear of the dwelling of Mr. Cole. Some of the brigands left the ranks in pursuit, and one, said to be Bennett, a silversmith, and resident of Detroit, taking the lead, rested his piece upon the fence which the doctor had just crossed, and fired. Bennett then turned to his party and said "you may go and take his sword, he will not run any farther." Several then proceeded to "finish" him, as they expressed it, and in doing so, mangled his remains in the most shocking manner. This minute statement of the transaction is given to correct a fabrication got up, either as an attempt at a miserable palliation of the brutal act, or for the purpose of effect, viz: "that the brigands had shot Dr. Hume, under the impression that he was Colonel Prince." After killing the doctor, they fired several shots at Morse, who had a most miraculous escape—one of their bullets passing through his hair. The others of the party in the wagon were made prisoners by the brigands.

On our forces reaching Sandwich, it was positively ascertained that no body of men had been seen either on the American side of the river, opposite Sandwich, or in the groves in the rear of the town, as stated by Col. Prince's

informants. Intelligence was also given by James Dougall, Esq., and other respectable inhabitants who had
been reconnoitering at Windsor, that the brigands re-
maining at that place certainly did not exceed one hundred men; and that they were evidently preparing to
leave it, as they had fallen back from the spot where they
had murdered Dr. Hume, to a position in front of the
store of Gardner & Babcock.   Col. Prince was made
acquainted with these facts and earnestly solicited ·by Mr.
Dougall and others, as he had now 200 men upon the
ground, to send up a force to dislodge the enemy. This
he refused to do, giving as his reasons that the report
could not be correct—that the party at Windsor must be
much stronger than represented—that his post was at
Sandwich and if he should leave it he would by so doing
subject himself to trial by a court martial, and the liabil-
ity of being shot. He further stated that he had on the
first alarm dispatched an express to Malden for some
regulars and a field piece, and that he did not think it
advisable to move against the enemy until their arrival,
which might be expected in two or three hours.   The

appearance of this reinforcement was now most anxiously looked for, as it was plainly seen that no movement would be made until it had arrived. In the meantime information continued to be received from many respectable individuals who had been closely reconnoitering, of the weakness of the enemy and their evident alarm
and dread of being attacked. It was confidently stated
that even fifty men could disperse or make prisoners of the
whole party; and Ensign Rankin, of the Provincial volunteers, solicited Col. Prince for that number, with whom
he gallantly volunteered to drive the polluting ruffians
from our soil. His request was denied—and the enemy
remained for hours in possession of the village without
any attempt being made to dislodge them; and were
actually permitted to march off at leisure, with drum
beating, and colors flying. After they had vacated Windsor, horseman after horseman hurried down to apprize
Col. Prince that they had retreated to the Windmills,
(their place of debarkation), and were escaping by canoes
to Hog Island; this intelligence, however, did not cause

Col. Prince to change his determination to remain at Sandwich until the arrival of the regulars.

When we had waited an hour or longer for the expected reinforcement a prisoner who had been wounded and taken after the engagement was brought into town. He was conducted, surrounded by several of our men, towards Col. Prince, who was then standing in the most frequented part of our main street.   As the prisoner approached he was told by one of the officers to make his peace with God, as he had but a few minutes to live.   The wretched man, holding up both his hands, pleaded most earnestly for mercy, but Col. Prince commanded him to be shot upon the spot, and the same officer who had at first addressed him, probably to disengage him from those by whom he was surrounded, ordered him to "run for his life"—and in an instant a dozen muskets were leveled for his execution.   At this moment Col. William Elliott, of the Second Essex, who chanced to be near at hand, exclaimed, "D—n you, you cowardly rascals, are you going to murder your prisoner."   This exclamation for one instant retarded the fire of the party, but in the next the prisoner was brought to the ground; he sprang again to his feet, and ran around the corner of a fence, where he was met by a person coming from an opposite direction and shot through the head. From papers found upon his person it appeared his name was Bennett. It is to be regretted that this painful affair took place in our most public street, and in the presence of several ladies and children, who had been attracted to the doors and windows by the strange events of the morning, but who little expected to witness so awful a tragedy. Another brigand named Dennison, also wounded and unarmed, was taken after the action and brought in during the course of the morning. Charles Elliott, Esq., who happened to be present when the prisoner was about to be shot by Col. Prince's orders, entreated that he might be saved to be dealt with according to the laws of the country; but Col. Prince's reply was, "D—n the rascal, shoot him," and it was done accordingly.

To the great satisfaction of our anxious people, about 11 o'clock a. m. a detachment of 100 men of the Thirty-fourth, under Capt. Broderick, a few artillerists and a field piece, under Lieut. Airey, and some forty or fifty Indians under Geo. Ironside, Esq., galloped into Sandwich. Waiting only a few minutes to inquire the state of affairs at Windsor, which place they were told was still in possession of the brigands, (although it had actually been evacuated long before), they proceeded at full speed up the road in search of the enemy. Col. Prince having by this time discovered that there were no brigands in the groves in the rear of the town, nor any crossing the river, nor any anywhere else in the neighborhood of Sandwich, except those which he had left in possession of Windsor, and those who might have rallied after he had recalled their pursuers—followed the regulars with the whole of his command and all the male inhabitants except some sixteen or eighteen men of the artillery company under Capt. Chewett. This small force with a nine-pound field piece, were posted at the north entrance of the town, and to it was committed the defense of the stores, ammunition, etc., etc., in the event of Col. Prince being again misinformed, and any attack from the groves in the rear, or from the opposite shore

being made upon the place. When Col. Prince reached
Windsor he was informed that one of the brigands was
lying wounded in the house of Mr. Wm. Johnson. The
man whose leg had been shattered by a musket ball had
been found by Francois Bâby, Esq., after the action, and
by his orders was removed to Mr. Johnson's, with a promise of surgical assistance. Col. Prince gave the order for
his execution, and he was dragged out of the house and
shot accordingly.

The regulars and artillery in wagons, and the Indians
on horseback, were by this time two or three miles in
advance of Col. Prince. They had discovered no enemy
at Windsor, and so continued the pursuit to the Windmills, where they found the reported escape of the brigands but too correct. Nothing could be seen of those
whom the militia drove to the woods, nor of those who
had so long held possession of Windsor, except one man
who was made prisoner, and five or six others who were
then crossing in canoes to Hog Island. The captured brig-
and made earnest appeals for mercy, to which Capt. Broderick replied, "You have fallen into the hands of a Brit-

ish officer." On discovering the canoe Lieut. Airey ordered the field piece to be unlimbered and a fire to be
opened upon the retreating rascals. Some capital shots
were made but without effect, until Lieut. Airey himself
pointed the gun, when one shot struck the canoe amid-
ships, just as it reached ice, and killed one man and severely wounded another.

When the brigands first commenced crossing to the
island they dismissed some of our men whom they had
carried prisoners from Windsor; the rest they put into
the Windmills and detained there until the last of their
party was ready to leave, and then dismissed them also.

As soon as Gen. Brady was apprised of the invasion
of our country he dispatched Maj. Payne with a detachment of United States troops and a field piece on board
the steamboat, to act as circumstances might require.
Maj. Payne, at the time the brigands were making their
escape in canoes, was crossing in the channel between
the island and our shore, and as it was afterwards ascertained, intercepted and made prisoners of a number,
whom he delivered to the authorities at Detroit.

Capt. Broderick, finding there was nothing further to be done, commenced his return to Sandwich, leaving the prisoners whom he had taken to be brought down under charge of a dragoon and some others. Col. Prince, after meeting the regulars on their return, continued his march to the Windmills, and about a quarter of a mile below them fell in with Broderick's prisoner. He ordered the man to be taken from the guard and to be shot upon the spot, which was done accordingly.

About the time Capt. Broderick had commenced his return the Indians had gone in pursuit of some of the enemy who had taken to the woods. After a sharp chase they succeeded in taking seven prisoners, one of whom in attempting to escape after being captured was fired upon, wounded and retaken. When the prisoners were first brought out of the woods the cry was, "bayonet them," but Martin, one of the Indian braves, replied, "No, we are Christians, we will not murder them—we will deliver them to our officers, to be treated as they think proper." They were then brought to Col. Prince, who had now commenced his return to Sandwich. When he had ar-

rived opposite the burning barracks he ordered the wagon
in which the prisoners had been placed to be wheeled
off the road. As soon as it had reached an open spot in
the rear of the ruins, he commanded the men be taken
out and shot.   At this critical moment Charles Elliott,
and Robert Mercer, Esqs., and the Rev. Mr. Johnson, and
Mr. Samuel James rushed forward and entreated Col.
Prince not to commit murder by shooting the prisoners,
but begged him to leave them to the laws of the country.
In making this appeal Mr. James made use of the em-
phatic language, "For God's sake, do not let a white
man murder what an Indian has spared."   Col. Prince
yielded to the entreaties of the gentlemen, remarking to
Mr. Elliott that he would hold him responsible for his interference, as his (Col. Prince's) orders were to destroy
them all.

By information received immediately after the flight
of the brigands it was known that a large number had
escaped to the woods. No party, however, was sent to
scour the neighborhood, nor were any guards stationed
on the shore of the river or Lake St. Clair to cut off re-

treat nor were the means of transportation removed by placing the canoes and boats under safe keeping. On the following day five or six gentlemen volunteers went out about fourteen miles and captured eight of the brigands. About thirty of the enemy succeeded in crossing in a body at the river St. Clair and arrived in Detroit on the following Friday, and parties of two to five continued to escape for several days, and even weeks after their defeat.

The number of the enemy killed in the engagement, with those afterwards shot, was correctly ascertained to be 32; and the prisoners taken, brought in and committed at Sandwich and Malden amount to the same number. The prisoners taken at Chatham are said to exceed twenty in number. Many of the misguided and guilty fugitives no doubt perished in the woods from cold, hunger and wounds. Our loss was four killed and four wounded— none mortally.

In closing this narrative it will not be deemed presumptuous to say that the greatest praise is due to Capt. Sparke, his officers and the Provincial volunteers for their gallantry and skill—not to add that the officers and men of the militia are entitled to our high consideration for their coolness, bravery and promptitude. The only opinion we will hazard, where we profess to state solely facts, is that the brigands flattered themselves they should be joined by our gallant Canadian militia men; we think they are by this time cured of so vain a delusion.

*Colonel John Prince was publicly condemned for the summary manner in which he disposed of the rebel prisoners, and the feeling became so pronounced that a commission was appointed to take proof of his acts and the causes leading up to the same. The evidence was taken at Sandwich and the deposition forwarded to the English government, and a strong effort made to convict him, but he had a powerful supporter in the Duke of Wellington, who at this time was Prime Minister, and who addressed the House of Lords in his behalf and he was acquitted. He was soon afterward appointed District Judge of Algoma and died some years ago at the Canadian Sault Ste. Marie.

---

*The defenceless state of Canada at the time of the rebellion and the desperate character of the rebels were among the principal arguments used in Col. Prince's behalf.

OLD BABY HOUSE, AT
SANDWICH, ONT.

PROMINENT MEN OF ESSEX.

———

1832.—Probably the most noted person that settled in Sandwich was the late Col. John Prince. He came from Cheltenham, a noted watering place in England, was a successful chancery lawyer, married, with four children, born in England. His object was to settle on a large tract of land in the then territory of Illinois, but finding the attractions so alluring in the way of climate, game, fish, etc., in the western district that he remained there, purchasing the homestead of the late George Jacobs, Esq., and subsequently several park lots adjoining the town of Sandwich, which constituted the so-called Park farm. He brought with him 75,000 guineas, and amongst his many and various accomplishments he was a keen sportsman and a splendid shot, had a fine breed of choice setters and brought with him several brace of English pheasants to breed from on his farm. A man of splendid

physique, about five feet ten inches in height, powerfully de-
veloped chest and shoulders and a voice of thunder, but
so controlled and modified that at times it filled the audience
with wonder at his powerful denunciations and his electric
flights of oratory. A striking type of Dan. O'Connell, the
renowned Irish patriot.

He had been in Sandwich but a short time when he asked
me if I would join him and show him the noted grounds
for game about Sandwich, which I gladly did, and I was
much edified in witnessing his well-trained dogs and his admirable shooting. After our day's sport, he invited me to
dine with him, which I accepted with much pleasure, and I
shall never forget the surprise and awkward position I was
placed in at the following incident. Arriving at his home
and seated in his parlor waiting dinner, and his charming
wife seated at her harp, which she played with artistic skill.
The servant, a bright-looking English girl (by instructions
from her master, of course), approached me first with a silver tray and on it a silver two-handled tankard filled with
foaming beer (home brewed). Rather taken aback at this
offer, I stared at the poor girl, and asked for a tumbler to

drink out of, which Prince noticed, and in the most kind, insinuating and cordial manner remarked, "My dear young friend, when an English gentleman invites his guest to partake of his hospitality his first desire is to honor him by his taking the first draught from the bowl, and the family follow." Thus assured, I seized it by the two handles and freely imbibed the flowing beverage with a high appreciation of the honor bestowed upon me, notwithstanding my narrow, unsophisticated ideas of Canadian gentility. After spending a pleasant evening, I left with an agreeable remembrance of the hospitality of my distinguished host. There was something so charmingly inviting in this remarkable man's address and conversation that it was no wonder he so soon became the idol of the people and gained his popularity. He was soon elected member of Parliament, was a very active one, and subsequently was appointed District Judge of Algoma, and died there and was buried at his own request on an island in front of his home on the St. Mary's river. So keen an appreciation had he of our Canadian shooting sport that a short time after settling in this country he sent to England and had made for him a double-barreled gun, in weight about twenty pounds, one barrel a smooth bore, to use with wire cartridges and kill from the top of the highest oak or elm a wild turkey at a distance of 150 or 200 yards, and the other a rifle bore with which he could bring down a buck on the run at 300 yards; and the balcony at the house of the Park farm is proof of his success, with its decorated wall of moose, elk and deer heads nailed to it as trophies. As a member of Parliament he was instrumental in having several popular and highly commendable acts passed—viz., master and servant act, game laws, cruelty to animals and for opening out and construction of the middle road in Maidstone township, etc., and at the same time building the Canard bridge near Amherstburg. Two years previous to his death he met with a painful and distressing accident in breaking in a young and powerful stallion. He was simple and careless enough to wind the chain halter round the thumb of his left hand, and a violent jerk of the colt tore it from the socket. It was said this frightful accident accelerated the cause of his death.

Nearly contemporary with this remarkable man was Arthur Rankin, born at sea (Atlantic), spent the days of his youth about Owen Sound, Collingwood and Little York, as chain bearer to his brother Charles, land surveyor, joined the Queen's Light Infantry at Toronto when sent to the Detroit frontier in 1838. Conspicuous in the part he took at the battle of Windsor, when he captured the flag of the so-called Patriots. His handsome, gallant and military air could not but attract the undivided admiration of the host of fascinating and attractive belles of the frontier, and one of the most prominent and brilliant of the brunettes met his fascinating smile, resulting in a clandestine marriage, to the surprise and astonishment of their numerous friends. Shortly after this he proceeded with a band of Indians from Walpole Island to England, where he attracted marked attention in the city of London from the extravagant and gorgeous display of his troop, driven by himself, as an Indian chief, in a van made for the purpose, with his team of six gorgeously caparisoned cream-colored horses drilled to the quick step of a brass band in attendance. Sold out to Catalin (Indian showman) for a large amount and returned to Canada, embarked in commercial, mineral and land speculations. Controlled and formed a company to develop the Bruce mines.

Elected member of Parliament for the county of Essex, appointed colonel of militia, and in 1863 formed the extravagant, though chivalrous scheme of raising a regiment of lancers to fight the battles of the Northern States. This step, however, proved unfortunate for him, as the Canadian government wisely thought it incompatible for him to fight for both countries in case of a collision between the two, so he lost his commission as colonel in the Canadian militia. However unfortunate in this instance and misguided in many others of his various enterprises, this must be said by his many friends and fewer enemies that a more polished, engaging, interesting and hospitable gentleman and a faster friend never pressed the soil of Canada than Arthur Rankin. When the late deputy treasurer, W. R. Wood, was obliged to leave the country as a defaulter, his beautiful home on the banks of the Detroit River was purchased by Col. Rankin and the proceeds of the sale of this property and all the personal effects of Wood were sacrificed to pay his indebtedness to the country. Rankin died at the Hotel Dieu Hospital in Windsor, on the 13th of March, 1893, and was buried in the Catholic Cemetery at Sandwich.

JOURNEY FROM LITTLE YORK TO SANDWICH IN 1827.

———

After spending some time at home in Little York in various occupations, my brother Charles, who was established at Sandwich then, paid a professional visit to Little York, and I was induced to follow and returned with him to Sandwich.

We left Little York, now Toronto, in the commencement of March, 1827, in a light dog cart that my father gave me, as also a four-year-old powerful horse named Pete, and with Charles' horse Rattler as leader and roads in a dreadful state, although at that time the most improved and best settled in Ontario. We reached Dundas (then the principal town at the head of Lake Ontario, Hamilton then not in existence, but became so not many years after, and taking its name from George Hamilton, one of its first settlers), where we found an exceedingly comfortable and well kept hostelry. The landlord's name I forget, but regret he is not mine now. We found boarding at this inn an old and esteemed friend, J. B. Ewart, then the most prominent business man in Canada West, and who shortly afterwards married the daughter of the Hon. James Crooks. After two days recruiting, we proceeded westward and reached Whithead's, another most comfortable inn, at the commencement of the then Burford woods.

From Burford to Oxford's Corners was very little more than a wilderness, and our next stopping place was at Ingersoll's inn. London was not in existence then, but soon became the county town afterwards of Middlesex. Our next stopping place was at Aljoes, in the Long Woods extending some fifteen miles, the road a corduroy one, huge logs thrown together without a covering, in the middle of which our iron axle-tree was broken and had to carry it on horseback five miles to the first blacksmith shop to have it spliced. Our next halt was at Gardner's Mills, in Mosa, who kept a house of entertainment, no liquor kept there. After leaving Gardner's and striking the River Thames again, came to the famous battleground, Moravian town, and soon after crossed the bridge in the Howard township, and followed the banks of the River Thames to its mouth through an old settlement. Stopped over night at an inn kept by F. Latti-boache, where stands the present lighthouse, and took the Lake St. Clair ice, though very unsafe, and followed it till we reached the Detroit river, and arrived at Sandwich after twenty-one days' travel from Little York.

NAVIGATION ON LAKE ONTARIO—1824.

I should have alluded before this to my earliest recollection of the state of navigation previous to this time.

The first steamer that entered Little York (now Toronto) Bay was the Frontinac, built at Kingston in 1817, commanded by Capt. McKenzie, R. N., 700 tons. Another steamer, called the Ontario, made her appearance, built at Sacketts Harbor, 230 tons, commanded by Capt. Malory, U. S. N. These were soon followed by the Martha Ogden, Am. & Queenstown, Can., Alciopie Can., Great Britain, Capt. Whitney, of Kingston. Among the sailing vessels were The Brothers, Capt. John McIntosh; Kingston Packet, Capt. Bill Bucket; sloop Duke of Richmond, Capt. Richard Oats, the two latter passenger boats between Little York and Niagara. More particularly have I reason to remember the Martha Ogden steamer, and but for my good qualities as a swimmer I would not be here to tell the tale.

On an evening of her expected arrival, in company with

my brother Charles and one or two others, we repaired to her wharf, and after the passengers had been landed we stepped on board and spent some time in a very jovial manner with the captain and a large party. Of course, the decanters were passed round freely, and notwithstanding my youthful age imbibed, if not as freely as the rest, to say the least, indiscreetly, as it proved. When about leaving the steamer the gang plank, which was placed aft of the wheel-house to the wharf, left a space of several feet from it, and, the night being pitch dark, I boldly placed my right foot upon it and the left one eight feet below, the water's edge, under which I floundered for dear life's sake. The alarm of a man overboard soon brought a crowd to the wharf, while I remained struggling to keep afloat, and luckily in doing so got my finger in a knot hole in a plank facing the wharf, to which I held on to until my brother Charles had himself let down, feet first, which I seized and was then drawn up completely sobered, and not a little thankful for my narrow escape.

AT SCHOOL IN ST. RAPHAEL'S IN 1825.

It was while at this college that the ordination of the first Catholic priests took place in Ontario—viz., the Rev. Angus McDonell, nephew of the bishop, who became parish priest at Sandwich and who planned and built the present beautiful Church of L'Assumption there. The Rev. Mr. Gordon, afterwards vicar-general at Hamilton; the Rev. Mr. Campion, Prescot; the Revs. Brenman, Cullan and Lawler, stationed in different parts of Ontario. The principal of the college was the Rev. W. P. McDonell, who succeeded the Rev. Mr. Gordon at Hamilton as vicar-general and who published the Catholic newspaper of that name. He had been a school-mate of the bishop in Spain, was ordained there and followed him to Glengarry and was appointed principal of the college to its close—a gifted scholar, elegant and refined in manner and a profound and earnest Christian. Died in Hamilton, Ont.

About the 1st of May, 1826, the bishop left St. Raphael's for Little York, and I accompanied him returning home. We drove in an open carriage, and between Lancaster and Cornwall stopped at an inn kept by Mr. Campbell, and, if I am not mistaken, not far from the battlefield of Chrysler's farm, when and where the bishop took an active part in 1812 as soldier and chaplain to the famous Glengarry Fencibles. If my memory is at fault with the locality of this place, I retain a vivid recollection of the sumptuous dinner served by mine host of cod's head and shoulders with oyster sauce, it being Friday, in respect to his lordship, and which I fully enjoyed. This noted hotel keeper not long afterwards kept the British American, foot of Scott street, Toronto, for many years after.

AN OLD-TIME BREEZE ON LAKE ERIE—SAILING IN 1831.

The Baby Mansion, Around which Cluster Historic Memories.

In the winter of 1831 I was sojourning in the rural town of Sandwich, under the roof of the old and venerable pile, the Bâby mansion, my place of nativity. There is something so truly interesting in this place, identified as it is with the past history of the country, that, although I have on more than one occasion alluded to it, I cannot refrain from adding this, my last tribute to its history. It was built about the middle of the last century and one can scarcely imagine nowadays the difficulties then experienced in accumulating the material and the labor to erect so well built a structure. There was no such thing as a saw mill or grist mills, except the scattered "moulins a vent" (wind mills) along the shores of the River Detroit. The nearest saw and grist mill by water power, even up to the year 1828, I believe, was McGregor's at Chatham, some fifty odd miles from Detroit, which served the wants of the inhabitants generally. The siding and all lumber required for use in construction of the building was cut out by a whip saw, such as we now see used only in the construction of vessels or ships, and every board was finished with a bead, and every wrought iron nail driven through a hole bored with a gimlet to avoid splitting. The house is about 40x50 feet in size, two and one-half stories in height, with a three-foot stone wall cellar, the size of the house, and as it was built for the northwest trade, it was made capable of holding 600 or more pipes of wine or liquors, which were then of the best quality in the world, and were brought from Montreal in "bateaux" (four-ton open boats), the same as all other merchandise for the northwest trade. They were brought as far as Queenstown in boats, then loaded in wagons and conveyed to Chippewa and again transhipped in bateaux, threading their way along the Niagara River and the shore of Lake Erie to their different points of destination —Detroit, Mackinac, Sault Ste. Marie, Green Bay, St.

Paul, etc. The frame work of the building was filled in with bricks and mortar; the beams and the sheathing were of oak, and the sills of doors and windows of walnut. In the hall was hung an iron hook, from which was suspended massive scales capable of weighing 2,000 pounds of furs—otter, beaver, buffalo, mink, etc. The roof is steep to shed the tempest blasts of snow and rain. It stands the silent witness of the cannon's roar on lake and field, (battle of Lake Erie and the taking of Detroit in 1813). Its walls, halls, and chambers have re-echoed the voices of Hull, Brock, Proctor, Harrison and Tecumseh. After the battle of the River Thames, where Tecumseh was killed, the father of the writer, Col. James Bâby, of the Kent militia, was taken prisoner and returned to Sandwich with Gen. Harrison, who occupied this house as his headquarters, and his humane and honorable treatment of the Canadians during this campaign was always held in grateful remembrance by them. This house has sheltered and entertained the mitered and ermined, and its doors were ever opened alike to the Huron and the habitant.

The surroundings were in keeping with the house; it
had a well stocked garden of the choicest fruits the climate could produce.   On October 3d, 1888, I measured
two of its pear trees over a hundred years old; the bon
chretian, grafted on the stock of the old French pear
tree, the other, the French pear tree itself.   They both
measured nine feet in girth, consequently about three feet
in diameter; in height seventy feet or more, and in full
bearing.   These first and tenacious emblems of the gos-
pel and cross brought here from France nearly two cen-
turies ago, nursed and cradled by the tender care of the
missionary fathers in wet moss, and planted and inter-
mingled with the primeval forest adorning both sides of
the Detroit River from source to mouth, irrigated by the
limpid waters of Superior and Huron, which flow on to
pay tribute to Niagara's fearful cliff, from whose caves
(wild nature's pealing organ) ascends in thunder's roar
and mingles with the rainbow's tinted spray, a pure and
holy incense, forever soaring to mark the finger of their
God.   These emblems then are gradually disappearing,
but in the archives of Loyola will live forever.   As did the

poet in bidding adieu to his native land so will I to thee, the place of my birth and say, "good night."

I find that I have been wandering, so will return to my subject, the "Breeze." At the time before mentioned (the winter of 1831) I was not particularly occupied, professionally or otherwise, and an idea struck me that money could be made by a sailing vessel. As there was one, unfinished, for sale on the stocks at Sandwich, I bought her, excepting a few shares, fitted her out and called her the Tecumseh. At that time an iron furnace, built by Fields & Cahoun, was in full blast in the township of Gosfield, and there was a great demand for pig iron freight by water to Toronto. I took a contract to deliver a certain quantity there, and sent the vessel through with a full cargo whilst I followed by steamer. On her arrival the crew mutinied. I paid them off, bought out the shares owned by the other shareholder through a generous act of my father, then inspector-general of Upper Canada, and trod the deck as boss. I had acquired a good deal of experience in my youth in Little York (now Toronto) Bay in the way of managing a skiff or sailboat, and often steered for the expert salmon fisher up the Don, Credit and Humber rivers, in pursuit of this king of the finny tribe. It is to be observed (en passant) that these now almost extinct fish, in former days, frequented these streams in schools of thousands, for the purpose of spawning, which took place in the months of September and October, and when then taken were almost worthless and could be bought for 20 cents each, after their long journey of 1,500 miles from the Gulf of St. Lawrence, mostly in our fresh, and to them tepid waters, streams and lakes, whereas, in the spring of the year, as high as $4 or $5 could be had for them. It was not only by boat they were caught, but in a more primitive way: The settlers in the neighborhood of these streams depending more or less upon gun, or rod (they were adepts at either) for fish or game, could be seen along the shore with a flambeau, made from the pitch pine roots and knots, burned in what was called a "light jack," made of iron, the size of a half bushel measure, fastened to a staff, which was driven in the bank at the edge of the stream, where the water ran swiftly over a rocky or pebbly bottom, two or three feet deep where a piece of white birch bark, four by six feet in size, had been sunk, weighted with stones; the unwary salmon, intent upon passing the rapid over this bark, was pierced and taken by the unerring spearman.

The widow of the late Col. George Denison, my informant, who resided at the first rapids of the Humber, told me that, "Oft in the stilly night" did she and her friends wile away many an hour in witnessing this interesting scene. All has to succumb, however, to the transmutation of time. What a melancholy reflection!

To think that this priceless fish has become now nearly extinct in our fresh waters, and the reason is obvious, for no fish equals the salmon for its love for pure and limpid streams, and they are now shut out from them by mill dams and the filthy water produced by various manufactories erected on them. To return to my subject, what, with my experience in salmon fishing and that acquired by sailing with Capt. Bill Bucket, in the Kingston packet, and Capt. R. Oats, of the sloop "Duke of Richmond," (the former announcing her departure by the

blast of a tin horn, six feet long, the latter by the yelp of
a four-pound swivel). I scarcely found myself capable
to sail or handle a vessel with compass and chart. It so
happened I met Prideaux Girty, a merchant and would-
be sailor from Gosfield. He was looking out for the
owner of the Tecumseh to ship his goods to Amherstburg, so I appointed him sailing master. I was to be
super cargo, and I hired a lad as cook, slush and bottle
washer. John Kirkpatrick, of Chippewa, merchant, dis-
tiller, miller and postmaster, then met me and asked me
to take a pair of millstones to Chippewa, which I agreed
to do. Having completed my cargo, I left Toronto with
a spanking north wind and had a quick run across Lake
Ontario to Port Dalhousie, the entrance to the Welland
Canal, and in two days climbed the ladder of the locks to
Port Robinson, on the Chippewa Creek, and arrived at
Chippewa; unloaded Kirkpatrick's millstones, received a
barrel of whiskey in turn for freight, hired a yoke of oxen
to tow us around the mouth of the Chippewa Creek into
the Niagara River—and I have often thought since that,
if the tow line had parted rounding the point, the Tecum-

CHIPPEWA CREEK,

seh's cargo, crew and barrel of whiskey in ten minutes
after would have gone over Niagara Falls and would
never more have been heard of, unless, perhaps, in the
debris of the whirlpool below. I again visited this spot
in 1845 on my wedding tour, and spent a few days with
the late Thomas Street, (my companion in youth), then
with his parents at their charming residence at the rapids just above the Falls of Niagara. On one occasion we
left for Buffalo, and took the steamer "Emerald," Capt.
Vanallan, at Chippewa with a party of friends on their
way to see McCready play "Richelieu" at Buffalo, and
passed through the present "cut" leading from the village
into the Niagara River, constructed to avoid the danger-
ous trip around the point. We got to Buffalo all night,
hired John Fox and Joe Ridley, two sailors from Colchester; left Buffalo and ran up the lake on the Canada
shore when it came on to blow from the southwest, and
fearing, as sailors say, a dirty night, ran to shelter under
Point Abino, about twelve miles from Buffalo.   It was
on this night I witnessed a most singular freak of nature.
I went on deck to relieve John Fox on watch at 12 mid-

night. The night was as dark as Erebus. Fox instructed me in my first duties, telling me to keep a strict eye to the weather, and in making my rounds I was to place my foot upon the anchor chain and I could easily find out if the vessel was dragging the anchor, and if so to let out more chain to give it a better grip.   I was thus occupied when to my utter astonishment and fear a bright light appeared, making everything as light as day, and casting my eyes to the mainmast discovered on the topmast a ball of fire about the size of an ordinary bucket. Alarmed at this, to me, unusual sight I hastened to the companion-way and called for the crew to come up, which they did, when old Joe Ridley exclaimed: "It's the Jack o' Lantern," (ignus fatuus), which vanished as soon as they appeared, but has never been effaced from my memory.

We left Point Abino the next morning and ran up the lake opposite Cleveland with a light easterly wind and drizzling rain.   Suddenly, about 5 p. m., a clear sky opened in the west, and in less than five minutes Lake Erie was a sheet of foam.   Before we had time to take

in sail the squall struck us, blowing the jib from its hanks
and carried it overboard and under the vessel. Letting go the fore and main sail sheets with a run, we put
the vessel before the wind under bare poles and let her
scud.   As night wore on the wind increased to a hurri-
cane and made things lively on board the Tecumseh. The
box stove broke loose and flew from side to side in the
cabin; the light in the binnacle was blown out; the man
at the wheel was lashed to the tiller and had to be relieved
every half hour, benumbed with sleet, rain and cold.   The
howling of the tempest and the hissing of the raging seas
as they unfurled their maddened white caps I'll never forget.   We succeeded at last in tying the tiger (stove) by
the leg to keep it from barking and biting, and were
crowded in the cabin, awaiting our fate, when at daylight the man at the helm cried out: "Land, ho!"   At
the time we were within two miles of Dunkirk lighthouse.
Then John Fox flew up the companionway to take in the
situation and proved equal to it. He cried out: "If we
can't get up the foresail we'll be in the breakers in less
than fifteen minutes."   We followed him and found the

halyards unreeved. He sprang to the rigging, reeved them and, with great difficulty (as the sail was frozen) we got up about twenty feet of it, brought the vessel to the wind, and that moment about ten feet of the bulwark of the weather bow was broached in by a heavy sea, but we held our own and crawled off the lea shore. The storm moderated rapidly and the sea went down. We recovered our jib and entered Buffalo harbor about 5 p. m., and found six vessels blown high and dry on Buffalo beach by the gale we had weathered. Having safely moored the vessel and left instructions for the damages to be repaired, I found my way to the then principal hotel, called the Eagle Tavern, and kept by old Ben Rathbun, and whilst at tea the alarm of fire was heard. Hastening to the scene the fire was discovered near the canal bridge, on Main street, I think it is, and the wind, again increasing to a gale, the fire was swept to several blocks in a few minutes. The annals of Buffalo (1832) will record it as one of the most destructive fires that ever occurred. I have every reason to remember it with great distinctness, for I never spent a more wretchedly uncomfortable and laborious night. Standing with a group of others and watching the progress of the flames, a violent slap upon the shoulders by a policeman warned me to fall into line and pass the fire buckets, and when exhausted with this another chap placed me at the twenty man-power engine to pump. In the meantime hogsheads of molasses, barrels of oil, etc., were rolled in the street and burst open, leaving us ankle deep in their contents. Thus did we work until broad daylight, when we were relieved. We repaired damages next day, and had a favorable run to Amherstburg, which we reached the 5th of January. Enough sailing for me.

THE RUNAWAY SLAVE.

In the year 1830 I was residing with my brother Charles in the old Bâby mansion, in the primitive and historical town of Sandwich. The house was built at the close of the last century and was the headquarters of Gen. Hull, when be invaded Canada in 1812; then in the year following he re-entered it as a prisoner of war (after the surrender of Detroit) with the illustrious Gen. Brock. It was the headquarters of Gen. Proctor, and the brave forest heroes, Tecumseh and Splitlog; and again after the battle of the River Thames Gen. Harrison occupied it as conqueror, and my father (the owner) as a prisoner of war, when so taken at the aforesaid battle while in command of the Kent militia, and was within pistol shot of Tecumseh, the bravest of the brave, when he fell mortally wounded. (In reality the house appears to be as sound and substantial to-day, October 8, 1895, as on the day it was finished.) We were keeping bachelors' hall, and, as a matter of course, experienced the difficulties attending housekeeping, as even now, for the want of proper help. In fact, servants in those days were out of the question, and fortunate it was if you could procure a person once a week to do the washing and scrubbing of the house. The ordinary routine of indoor work was done by the mother and daughters, and that of the outdoor work by the father and sons, even among the most respectable and refined of the community; and I question very much whether there is half the comfort, pleasure and happiness with our present servants now as then without them.

These various occupations embraced all manner of work but great store was placed on the successful raising of fruit and gardening. In fact the mainstay of the household, and what constituted the greatest delicacy in the vegetable line, was the asparagus, and this delicious succulent when propagated as it should be with a deep, rich mould for a top dressing, and cut when the pale and purple bulbs of an inch or more in diameter have made their appearance, and with a sharp and pointed sawbladed knife inserted three or four inches below the surface was quite a different sort of vegetable to that now generally seen exposed in our markets, more like grass going to seed than anything else.

The mild and genial spring showers in the month of May that brought this vegetable to perfection was accompanied with another (as great a delicacy) namely, the snipe, which in early days were to be found along the marshes bordering the Detroit River at and below Sand-

wich and the swales back of it, where a bountiful supply was always to be had by the keen sportsman
in the proper season. To commence my story, it was on
a balmy morning in the month of May when occupied in
our garden cutting asparagus, that a young man approached us and inquired if we wanted to engage a servant. Strongly prepossessed with his appearance, we
asked him where he came from, to which he replied that
he had run away from his master in Kentucky, had arrived the night previous in Detroit, crossed the river into
Canada as soon as possible, and was recommended to
us for employment.

Strange, I thought, that he had ever been a slave; his
finely-chiseled features and bright hazel eyes were not
those of a negro in the slightest degree, and save the
slight shade of his bronzed complexion, he could at most be
classed a quadroon. "How did you make your escape?"
we inquired. "In the dead of the night I mounted my
master's fleetest horse, passed the line in Ohio, and travelled on the underground railroad (a cordon of abolition-
ists; plainly speaking, scattered through the state, who suc-

coured and aided these unfortunate serfs in their flight), got to Cleveland and the rest has been told." "What was your occupation?" he was then asked. "My master hired me to a stone and brick mason, and when master of my trade and of age took building contracts, made lots of money, and so I left him with barely clothes to cover me, as you see. In my youth I was brought up to do all kinds of work, now in the kitchen, then in the garden, and again in the stable as groom. My mistress, being a French lady, prided herself on being a famous cook, and taught me how to prepare game and vegetables in the proper way." "Cést le garcon q'ill nous faut, engage le," I said to Charles in French. "The boy we want, hire him." No sooner said than done. Turning to him I said, "Well, then, try your skill in gathering up the cuttings of the asparagus." He followed me to the kitchen, and as we passed through the porch, I pointed out to him six brace of snipe, and desired him to prepare them, and mind not to remove the trail! It is needless to say he implicitly obeyed instructions, and had them served on toast and done to a turn. Andrew, for such was his name, proved a treasure. Respectful, cleanly, capable, lithe and active as a panther. We became much attached to him, and he to us. Some time elapsed, six months or so, when one morning while we were engaged in my brother's office writing up briefs, a knock was heard at the door, and the knocker desired to come in. A tall, slender person, with broad brimmed white felt hat, a cord and tassel in place of a hat band, dressed in Kentucky grey and the type of a Southern planter, addressed Charles, without taking off his hat, and asked, "Are you the proprietor here?" "In our country," replied Charles, "we are accustomed when past the threshold to uncover our heads; when you do so I will answer you." A crimson flush suffused his visage, and with a reluctant air he removed his hat. "Be seated, sir," said Charles, and in so doing he, the stranger, drew forth a cigar case and proffered each of us one, remarking at the same time, "I hope it will not be offensive to you to light a cigar." "Not at all, sir," we said, at the same time declining his offer. "I have reason to believe you have a runaway slave in your employment, and being a horse thief, I suppose you would be glad to get rid of him. In Michigan I could claim him, but in Canada your laws are different, I am told." "Decidedly so," was Charles' answer. Now continued the planter, "If the matter of two thousand ($2,000) dollars is an inducement, will you both lend me your aid in securing him?" Astonished at this proposition, Charles replied, "We don't barter in human flesh in Canada; your proposition I look upon as an insult, and the sooner you get out of this country the better for you." As he was about to leave, I said, "Hold on for a minute; if Andrew consents to go with you, all right; if not, he remains with us." So, hastening to the stable, I found Andrew busy grooming our horses (and a better pair never were saddled). "Andrew," I said, "do you know Mr. T., of Kentucky?" "Yes, sir," he replied. "He is in the office now and wishes to see you." If a thunder clap had unroofed the stable he could not have shown more terror. Dropping his currycomb and brushes, he exclaimed, "Great Heavens! My old master! What will become of me, Master William?" "Fear not," I said to him, "you are as safe here as in the fortress of Quebec, as far as the law is concerned, and you have many friends to protect you while with us. Come on, and meet him face to face; we'll take care of you."

Thus assured, we entered the office together. The Kentuckian, with an eagle eye fixed upon him, said: "Andrew, do you know me?" "Yes, sir, I know you too well." "What became of my favorite horse, Sweepstakes, that you stole from me?" "Sir, I never stole your horse. I used him as my best friend to gain my liberty. He was not saddle-galled, for I rode him bareback, and when he carried me twenty-five miles I dismounted on the road he was accustomed to travel, took the bit from his mouth, secured the bridle around his neck, turned his head homeward, and I am as sure that he reached it as I am that I fled from it." "You will not return with me, then?" "Never! The punishment I would receive at your hands would be death." "That's enough, Andrew; go now to your work," I said. Exit Andrew, exit planter, and as the latter left the door, grinding his teeth, he muttered, "I'll fix him." A short time after this interesting interview, Andrew re-entered and said, "I'm not safe here;

and I'll get further into the interior of the country. I thank you sincerely for your kindness and friendship, but I feel that you would be in danger as well as myself, if I remained. You little know his desperate character. I have seen him brain a colt that would not follow him without a halter." "You must do nothing of the kind," said Charles. "During the day there is no danger; at night there may be. We'll fit up the room at the left hand of the stair landing; keep the key in your pocket; make your bed there; load the two single and double-barreled guns you will find in the room with swan shot, and if anyone dares to open the door or window, blow out his infernal brains." These precautionary instructions were carried out to the letter. "There was a sound of revelry by night with pipe" and bowl, for a fortnight after in the old ancestral hall, 'till one or two in the morning keeping vigils with several friends in Andrew's defense, when it ceased, and we were tired out.

It so happened that our every movement through spies was watched, and it was discovered that usually on a Sunday Andrew was left at home alone. Fortunately

for him on this occasion, Charles was unavoidably detained there, and was engaged in reading in the front
room with doors and windows wide open, when an unusual sound struck his ear as if brickbats or rocks were
striking against the board fence and the side of the house.
It would appear that the man with the broad brimmed
white hat had hired five desperadoes in Detroit to kid-
nap Andrew while we were at church.

They crossed the river in a rowboat and landed it immediately in front of the old mansion, some one or two
hundred yards from the house.   Andrew had gone to
the baker's for a fresh loaf of bread, and on his return
met the six ruffians awaiting him in the yard.   In a flash
he took in the situation, armed himself with two or three
stones lying loose in the yard, and made for the stable
door, which was standing wide open.   It was the noise
of these stones striking on the fence that drew Charles'
attention to the yard, and observing the knot of scoundrels endeavoring to tie Andrew hand and foot, he seized
the handle of an axe close by, and, bareheaded and in
shirt sleeves, went at them with the will of a tiger.

HE WENT AT THEM WITH
THE WILL OF A TIGER.

Surprised at this unexpected attack Andrew found himself relieved of two or three of them, (and the assurance of help gave him redoubled strength), and so mingled in the fray that it was doubtful who had the best of it. At this moment a cavalcade of horse carts and cavalry men hastening home from church (in a cloud of dust, and with the racket of a tempest), passed hard by, and jumped from their carts and dismounted their horses to see what the row was about.

Panic stricken at this invasion it did not take long for the kidnappers to shake the dust from their feet and, running to their boat, as if the devil was after them, they shoved from the shore, and were soon across the river. It was at this stage of the affair that I arrived from church and met Charles and Andrew at the gate, a sorry looking pair, truly; covered with dirt and blood, the clothes nearly torn from their backs, faint and exhausted, but neither seriously hurt. This was sufficient proof that there was no safety for him to be with us and the next day Andrew was paid off, a subscription was made up among our friends, and he was advised to go to Toronto by stage. He was supplied with letters of recommendation and when Charles met him repeatedly for several years after, he was ever grateful for our sorely tried friendship, and remained contented and prosperous in his place of refuge.

JOURNEY TO LITTLE YORK (NOW TORONTO) IN 1833.

The sad and unexpected news of our father's death in the town of York (the present city of Toronto) on the 19th of February, 1833, caused the hurried departure of myself and brother Charles from Sandwich. On the evening of the 23d we reached Chatham with good sleighing, where we put up at an inn kept by one Claude Cartier, immediately on the bank of the River Thames and opposite the present Rankin House. Chatham was then but an insignificant hamlet. Sauntering about while supper was getting ready, we entered the sitting room, where we

HE WAS BADLY
FROSTBITTEN.

observed the rather unusual sight of a person seated in an arm chair with his feet in a tub of water and enveloped in a blanket from head to foot. Asking the landlady who this person was she replied that he was a stranger and was badly frostbitten. A natural feeling of sympathy prompted us to approach him, and we asked him whence he came and how he came to be in this pitiable plight.

"My name," he replied, "is Vidal, a captain in the Royal Navy. I arrived in Little York (Toronto) from England about a month ago, leaving my wife and young family at an hotel there for the purpose of visiting, and perhaps settling in this part of Canada. I arrived here by stage yesterday morning, and engaged the landlord Cartier as a guide, who told me that he was (as he appeared to be) familiar with the country for forty miles around. My intention was to examine some lots of land in the seventh concession of the township of Raleigh, and after taking a hasty breakfast started off on foot, making a bee line through the unbroken forest with not even a clearing in sight. We found the lots, but not until daylight was waning, and a heavy snowstorm had set in. All traces being thus hopelessly obliterated we soon lost our proper course homeward, and found that we were traveling in a circle (invariably the case with a lost woodman). In this emergency Cartier proposed that I should remain behind and he would attempt alone to find his way to the river whence he could return with some conveyance to take me back to Chatham. As I was pretty well used up I consented, but he informed me that I should be buried in snow to keep from freezing. To this I agreed, and the storm having abated, Cartier, guided by the north star, found his way out to the river, whence he returned to within a short distance of the place where he had left me, and found me walking about briskly, having become very nervous and restless in my snow tomb, and fearful of the wolves, which I preferred meeting on foot. Hastening to the sleigh which he had provided we arrived here, when I found that I was severely frostbitten, and instead of rubbing me with snow they put me into this tub of warm water, which I think makes matters worse." We then asked him if we could be of any service. "Certainly you can," he replied. "As I can't write and will not be able for some time to come," he replied, "will you please drop a line to my poor wife and tell her as gently as possible how I am situated." We told him that we were making all haste to get there, and would call on Mrs. Vidal and inform her as he desired. This seemed to cheer him up and give him great relief. What was to us surprising was the courage and fortitude of this afflicted British sailor. Thrown upon the mercy of strangers, suffering excruciating agony his pluck and endurance never for a moment forsook him. He related to us the following incident. "When I was in Paris, France, last and strolling along the Boulevard St. Germain, I entered a cafe and ordered a dejeuner a la fourchette, and seating myself outside, two elderly gentlemen approached, and seated themselves at a table next to me; one said to the other: "You are a martyr to rheumatism, you tell me; is it painful?" "Well, I should say so," he replied. "I can only compare it to one putting his finger in a vise, and give it one turn, that's it." "Oh," replied the other, "that's nothing like gout, with

which I am tormented; give the vise another turn, and
that's the idea." "Well," said the captain, "had I those
two old codgers here I would tell them to give that vise
another turn, and that is frost bite."

On our return from Little York eight or ten days after,
when passing through the Dorchester woods, we met a
double (boxed) sleigh, in which we observed as it was
passing a man lying at full length on his back, covered
with buffalo robes and blankets, his head only visible.   It
turned out that this was Capt. Vidal.   He told us he was
getting on all right, and he hoped to be soon out again.
He was much pleased to hear that we had seen Mrs.
Vidal, who was quite well, and that we had delivered
his message.   Two years after this I happened to be at
the Windsor and Detroit crossing, and observed a small
craft anchored in the stream opposite what was then
Pierre St. Amour's inn, now the British American hotel,
and I asked Pierre to whom the craft belonged.   "To
Capt. Vidal, of Sarnia," he said, and the captain shortly
after making his appearance, I asked him if he remem-
bered me.   "I don't know you from Adam," he replied.

"Well, Captain," I rejoined, "I shall never forget you, and your venture in the Raleigh woods, and the figure you cut in Cartier's washtub!" "Ah," said he, "I now remember you distinctly, and the adventure you refer to, and our meeting in the Dorchester woods. On that occasion it took me four days to reach York, and I never left my sleigh during that time, as I found it much more comfortable than the wretched bedrooms at the taverns where there was no fire. The driver took good care of me during the day, and his bulldog slept in the sleigh and guarded me at night. On my arrival at York I sent for Dr. Widmer, a celebrated army surgeon settled in Little York, who, after examining me, pronounced my case a serious one. I said to him, 'Doctor, I am an old sailor, and would like to have as much of my hands saved as would haul in a rope or hold a tiller.' He did so, and brought me through, as you see," (exposing his right hand, with part of his thumb and four fingers gone). He did not show me his left hand or his feet; probably they fared a little better. He had purchased a farm and was settled at Sarnia, adjoining the town, and eventually became collector of customs at that port. (Father of the present senator.)

On our journey and on our return home we stopped at an inn in the Long woods with the sign "The Travellers' Home," and drove directly to the stable, where we found the landlord, who apparently was in a very bad humor. "What's up?" we asked him. "Oh," he replied, "I never was in such an infernal stew in all my life. Last night I was here in the stable doing up my chores, when my wife, whom I had left alone in the house, came rushing in, exclaiming, 'John, run quickly to the house, for the devil is there, sure!' Arming myself with my pitchfork, I hastened to the house and entering the barroom found the devil there, sure enough, facing me, with his back to the fire, clothed in a suit of sheepskins, with the wool on from head to heels, with a ram's head so dressed that the shape was perfectly preserved, the horns being well set up, and two glaring glass eyes the size of a silver dollar. 'Who and what the devil are you?' I asked him. 'Why, what's the matter with you?' he replied, 'and what's all this fuss about? Can't a man in this free coun-

"WHO, AND WHAT THE DEVIL ARE YOU?"

try dress as he pleases in this blasted climate of yours?
I see folks driving about wrapped in bear, buffalo and
wolf robes, 'why not I in sheep skins?' and throwing off
his suit and taking a seat before the open fireplace as
cool as a cucumber, ordered his horse to be put up, (he
had tied him to the signpost), to wash him with cold
water, rub him dry and bed him up to his belly in straw,
to prepare supper for him immediately, and ordered a hot
whiskey punch, to make him warm, all done according
to his directions. At night he ordered a tub of cold
water up to his room to take a bath before retiring to
bed. No fire and thermometer at zero. Next morning
after his breakfast he called for his bill, in which I had
charged him for extras for his horse and himself. He
flew into a towering rage at this, and said, 'Sir, you are
a knave and an extortioner, and I shall haul you up
before the first magistrate that I can find,' and strapping
on his sheep skins strode out to where his horse was
tied to the signpost. My wife making her appearance at
this moment, said to me, 'John, receipt that man's bill
and let him go, for he may give us a deal of trouble.'

So stepping up to him I said, 'Here is your bill, receipted, sir; but should you ever come this way again, give my house a wide berth, for if you don't I'll pepper you with a dose of buckshot, and there is no judge or jury that will find me guilty for shooting a wolf in sheep skins.'"

This eccentric individual was a brother of the late Col. Talbot, and he was then on his way to visit his brother, whose home was on the banks of Lake Erie, and not far from St. Thomas. I never heard if he ever paid his bill; but of course he did, for this class of individuals, though rough and cranky, are seldom dishonest.

VISIT TO COL. TALBOT IN 1841.

My first glimpse of this remarkable man was in the winter of 1820, when I was 8 years old. He was then a guest of Sir Perigrine Maitland, Lieutenant-Governor of Upper Canada. So well-known and distinguished a person could not make his appearance in Little York

(now Toronto) without notice, and particularly did he attract attention to his extraordinary winter dress. Seated
by the side of Lady Sarah Maitland in a sleigh, and
driving along King street in his sheepskin coat and cap,
with its sheepskin tail of eight or ten feet long wound
round his neck to serve as a muffler, with the end trailing
by the side of the sleigh. But when this garb was thrown
off and he made his appearance in parlor or drawing-
room, how changed his appearance!—the very type of an
aristocrat, a handsome and thoroughbred nobleman.
What a jolly time must these old soldiers have had toasting their shins before a blazing fire of billets of maple,
beech, or shag-bark hickory wood, with pipe alight and
flagon of good old Absalom Shades (of Dumfries, now
Galt's) whiskey at 20 cents per gallon, and fighting their battles in the peninsula over again—Salamanca, Tores Vidras,
Badajos, etc., etc., winding up with Quatre Bras and
Waterloo, and the thrill when they heard Napoleon cry
out, "Sauve qui peu,"—"run who can," and interlarded
with such questions and answers as this: "Well, Talbot,
what think you will Canada be one hundred years from

now?" Talbot replies, "It's pretty hard to say, but one thing is certain—I won't give an acre of my 100,000 to any chap who will not swear allegiance to the old flag," etc., etc.

Col. Talbot landed on the 21st of May, 1803, at Port Talbot. Terms were that for every settler whom he located on fifty acres he should himself be entitled to 200 acres. The grant to each settler was afterwards increased to 100 acres. I was always under the impression that he served in the Peninsular war, but was mistaken. He was settled in Canada at that period.

Having lost sight of him from that year (1820) until the year 1841, an opportunity offered to renew our acquaintance, and having occasion to pass his residence in company with my brother Charles on our way to St. Thomas, our attention was drawn as we approached it to the remains of an old hedge fence planted alongside of the road, grown up at intervals to full sized forest trees, presenting a most neglected and unsightly appearance. Hitching our horses to the gate, we proceeded to the house, a couple of hundred yards from the road, which was situated on the bank, and fronting Lake Erie, and mounting a flight of steps leading to the kitchen, found ourselves on a gallery extending the length of the house. Inquiring of the servant at the kitchen for Col. Talbot, we were directed to proceed to a door at the other end of the gallery, and passing an open window, were saluted in a very gruff voice with his usual salutation, "What do you want?" Brought up all standing with this extraordinary interrogation, and trying to collect our senses, I ventured to reply, "A proper respect and a high regard for a friend of the late James Bâby, of Toronto, our father, has induced us to call on you." "That being the case, gentlemen, I am only too glad to see you. Proceed to the door and I'll let you in," and doing as he desired, and opening it, a swarm of geese, turkeys, ducks and fowls made for it. Still holding the knob of the door, he desired us to quickly enter, and slamming it with a bang, closed them out. This place served as a kind of store-room, where he kept all manner of farm products, and from which he fed his poultry. From this apartment he led us into his office or sittingroom, and having been seated, he thus addressed us: "You will, I hope, pardon me, gentlemen, for saluting you in that uncere- monious way, but the fact is, I am so pestered with these land grabbers who squirt their vile tobacco juice in every direction that I find it impossible to endure it, and I have adopted this plan of transacting all my business, through this open window. You will, I hope," he continued, (it being nearly 1 p. m.), "do me the pleasure of staying to dine with me. Not much choice in the country, you know. Excepting ham and eggs and poultry, there is little else." "Nothing better," we replied. "But, Col- onel, you must excuse us; we are in a hurry to get on to St. Thomas." "Well, a glass of old port or brandy will do us no harm," and descending into his cellar, soon re- appeared with a bottle in each hand, and after regaling ourselves and about to depart, led us into his store-room to show us the products of his sheep-farming, and cer- tainly if one could be a judge of such articles as bolts of cloth and flannels, and blankets of softest texture, the dis- play would have given credit to the best woolen factory in the country. From this room he led us into another

elegantly furnished apartment, hung with crimson velvet
paper, Turkey carpet and furniture to match. "This," he
remarked, "is my sanctum sanctorum. When my lady
friends visit me this is their room"—and nothing could exceed as a rural scene the view from its open window—
perched upon a hill of some 100 feet in height, and overlooking a meadow of twenty or thirty acres, with its
flock of snow white sheep quietly grazing, and girt with
a belt of forest trees still untouched by the ruthless axe.
Our visit ended we left the Colonel with many thanks
for his cordial and hospitable reception.

A rumor prevailed in Canada that this eccentric man
had been disappointed in some love affair in the old country, and he made up his mind to lead the life of a recluse
in the one of his adoption, and vowed eternal celibacy.
He carried that out, but at what a heavy charge, for he
burdened himself with all the cares of his household, doing the most menial work about it, even to the milking
of cows and making butter. How sad and melancholy
a reflection when one thinks of the awful sacrifices made
in Canada in those days by such men as Talbot, John

Prince, of Sandwich; Deblackyears, Vansittarts, Grahams,
Lizars and Alexanders, of Woodstock; the Dunlaps, of
Goderich; Crooks and Hydes, of Plympton; Jones, Fath-
orms, Vidals, Wrights and Sutherlands, along the shores
of Huron and river St. Clair, and a thousand others lost
to memory. Nursed and cradled in the lap of luxury, accustomed to all the refinements of civilized life, with ample means, then abandoning their comfortable homes in
the old country (many of them with grown up sons and
daughters fit to grace a throne), and scattered like wild
pigeons throughout the length and breadth of Canada's
then wilderness, to encounter a life of toil, privation, disappointment and sorrow. The result could be easily fore-
told. In less than three-quarters of a century they have
been swept away, and scarcely a vestige left behind. After
clearing up their farms and beautifying their country
homes, their means were exhausted, and at that time
no market to dispose of what they had to sell, which
they were as unfit to do as to black boots or sweep chim-
neys. Consequently the sturdy, iron-fisted, economical
and laborious field hand often became the owner of the

farm he helped to log and clear up. The difference between gentility and well directed labor.

These distressing events could not possibly have trans-
pired without leaving in the province an indelible stamp
behind them, and what was that?   Unswerving loyalty
to the British flag (many of them had been in the army
and served during the rebellion of '37 and '38 in Canada), the soul of honor in all their dealings, educated
and refined in their manners, and many of them became
from necessity useful servants in the civil or municipal
service.

How different a row to hoe had the U. E. Loyalists
and their descendants, as also their fellow settlers of
French, English, Scotch and Irish descent.   They were
"to the manor born." Inured and trained in dire necessity, their wants were few, and depended upon themselves to supply them. Their neighbors helped to build
their log houses and barns.   A genial climate and a
fruitful soil, which they loved, supplied them with their
necessary wants, and as time rolled on the country improved and supplied them with luxuries they never

dreamed of. But the greatest boon attained was education, and following it moral and religious training. Hence there is no portion of the habitable globe that can boast of a more sturdy, hardy and intelligent race of beings and a more favored soil and climate than Canada and its people. All it wants is good, stable government, with honest, liberal minded, intelligent men at the helm, and well can she then bid defiance to the restless croakers who are anxious and willing to sell their birthright for a mess of pottage.

AN UNEXPECTED VISIT FROM AN OLD SCHOOLMATE.

In perusing the interesting and highly valuable book, "Mrs. E.'s Ten Years in Canada," what scenes of my youth are not vividly called to my memory; one in particular. When about ten years of age there were few persons of any note I was not acquainted with in Little York, and most certainly one that I have never for-

gotten. He was merging from youth into early man-
hood, perhaps twenty or twenty-two years of age, about
five feet nine inches in height, well-knit frame, lithe and
active as a panther. His countenance as remarkable as
his physique. His wavy hair was auburn. His large
blue eyes were prominent, his complexion as fair as that
of a blonde of eighteen; was noted for his love of manly
sports, of fishing, shooting and boating, and a lover of
song and music. His delight was to roam among the
Indians, camped on the island, or on the banks of the
beautiful Don, whose vales and meadows are so picturesque.

He was employed as a clerk in the old Upper Canada bank, I believe the first one in Ontario, and lived
in a charming cottage near the Don. His great delight
was to man his northwest bark canoe with a picked crew
and race with the steamer "Canada" for miles in reaching her wharf.

Unfortunately, his only domestic female companion
was one of questionable reputation. As time wore on
a deficiency in the bank occurred, a meeting of the bank

directors was called and the guilt was fastened upon him.
A messenger was dispatched to his home, but the bird
had flown, and the messenger informed that he had left
early in the morning in his bark canoe. It was at once
conjectured that he had crossed the lake (Ontario) at the
nearest point to the United States and Capt. Richardson, of the steamer Canada, was dispatched by the bank
directors in pursuit of the fugitive, and overhauled him
near Fort Niagara, and upon ordering him to surrender, he stood up in his canoe and deliberately swallowed
the contents of a vial of laudanum.   Capt. Richardson
immediately returned with his prisoner to Little York,
and stopping at the garrison, took on board the surgeon
of the regiment, stationed there, and with the aid of a
stomach pump, ejected the poison.   While the patient
was in convulsions, and from which he recovered, was
tried and found guilty, and banished from the country.

No event that had ever occurred in the town had
proved such an astonishing and painful sensation.

A short time after his banishment he committed a for-
gery on the bank's cashier by signing his (the cashier's)

name to a draft; was tried and found guilty and imprisoned in Detroit's jail, situated at this time where the public library now stands.   The woman followed him and
was his constant visitor while in prison.   My brother
Charles, who was living with my uncle, Baptiste Bâby in
the old mansion in Sandwich, (still standing), hearing of
his incarceration, and having been one of his old school-
mates in Little York, called to see him, and felt deeply
in his misfortune and disgrace, and contributed to his
wants and comforts pending his trial.

I had paid a visit to Little York a short time before
this and had but just returned to Sandwich, when Charles,
in a confidential way, broached the subject I am about
to relate. "Who do you suppose paid me a visit last
night? Our old schoolmate, F. R.   I had retired to
bed," he continued, "and windows wide open from excessive heat, and about four a. m. (my lamp still burning), I heard my name called softly several times, and
putting my head out of the window heard him say in a
suppressed tone of voice, 'Is that you, Charley?' and I
replied, 'Yes, who are you?' And he said, 'Let me in,

quick. I am a friend.' So I slipped on my pants and slippers and descended the stairs, let him in and conducted him to my room upstairs. When brought to the light his appearance appalled and frightened me. A red silk handkerchief tied around his head, with ends hanging down his back, his short blanket coat on, and around his waist the useful sash, under which was stuck a butcher knife and in his stocking feet (he lost his blanket shoes in the marsh), and his story added to my consternation. I will repeat it in his own words.

For a fortnight past I led the turnkey to believe I was partially insane, and kicked up a d—l of a row in my cell, played on my flute (he was an excellent player) and hammered on the window sill, and my female friend supplied me stealthily with what I required. First, we were allowed to walk in the corridor of the prison, and with a piece of dough I took the impression of the keyhole of my cell door and with a piece of pewter or zinc hammered a key to fit it. I then cut a piece out of my blanket coat tail, and made a pair of slippers to avoid noise, chose a dark and stormy night for the purpose and about two a. m. rolled up

my blanket coat, tied it to one end of my sash, and started
for the end of the corridor where slept the turnkey near the
door. I had made up my mind to sell my life dearly if interrupted, and held the knife aloft, this is it (showing me a
butcher knife), and had he attempted my arrest he would
have felt its keen blade; approaching the door I felt for the
lock, which fortunately was unlocked, and loosening the
clasp it fell, and awoke the turnkey, who, sitting on his
haunches in bed, demanded "Who is there?" I could hear
my heart beat, and suppressed my breath; I held my knife
ready to destroy my victim if he attempted to seize me.
The howling and racket of the wind deceived him, and turning in his bed, he soon again slept and snored. I then
quietly opened the door sufficiently to let me pass through,
and mounting the stairway like a scared monkey, was soon
in the upper story of the old jail, which was surrounded
by a row of pointed cedar pickets about 15 feet
high.   Unloosening my sash, with one end of it
tied to the blanket I threw the latter from
an open window over the picket fence some six or
eight feet from me, and holding on to the end of the sash

jumped clinging to it. I then hauled myself hand over hand to the top of the fence, and dropping down outside, made for the river, and when opposite here, now Clark's dock, stole a skiff and landed nearly opposite, and not knowing the road to the river struck the marsh and waded through it, up to my hips, as you see. ·Now, said Charles, here was a dilemma that perplexed me and which would have puzzled a Philadelphia lawyer, as to what was to be done. I could not keep him with safety to myself, or him either, so I got him to clean himself up of his marsh mud, dressed him in a suit of my own clothes, and called with him on a confidential friend, and had him stowed away in the garret of his fowl house, where he can neither stand up or walk, but is crouched like a tiger in his lair. It was in this hole, which I climbed up to the next day on a short ladder, that I had my first glimpse of him since I had last seen the dashing, gay and festive Lothario in Little York! His wild and glaring eyes, and distended nostrils, and trembling voice, attested the soul-harrowing fear he labored under, so we soon left him with the promise to see him soon again. As we well knew, the

authorities in Detroit were wide awake and came over in
squads in search of the culprit, but he was so well concealed that he remained undiscovered, and shortly after
midnight with our aid he left Sandwich, through the back
woods, bound for Moravian town, an Indian village near the
famous battle ground on the River Thames, and after a few
days rest there started for another Indian village (Muncy-
town) in the township of Delaware, not far from London,
thence to Little York again, but Canada had ceased to
protect him, and again he got back to the United States,
was arrested, tried, incarcerated in Auburn's State prison
for life, and where by his prepossessing appearance, his
courtly and gentlemanly manners, he so ingratiated himself
in the good will of its managers, that he became usefully
employed there, until by some unlucky chance, he fell down
stairs and broke his neck.

Note.—In my brother's frequent visits to the jail he so
well informed himself as to the locality of the house that
otherwise he never would have reached it.

VISIT TO THE VILLAGE OF WICKWIMIKONG, MANITOULIN ISLAND.

On a sultry evening in the month of August, 1864, I was seated on my veranda in Sandwich, watching the vapors from my favorite T. D. pipe as they gently ascended and assumed various forms (suggestive of building castles in the air) when my meditations were suddenly interrupted by the appearance of my old friend, J. R. B., of Milwaukee, who cordially joined in this agreeable pastime, and the following subject was broached:

"I have just returned," he commenced, "from a trip in the Lake Superior region, in search of timber limits, and copper, gold or silver mines, accompanied by Mr. L. (a noted geologist of New York), and on our return home passed through the great Manitoulin Island, and on our passage through while skirting the shores of South Bay, on the southern portion of the island came in sight of a promontory of singular and striking appearance on its shore, as white as snow and resembling an old ruined castle, and on our near approach to it composed (as the geologist thought) of white limestone or marble in layers of two, six and twelve inches in thickness, and a shelf landing of the same rock, where a seventy-four-gun ship could be moored directly alongside of it." So striking and favorable an impression did this rock produce on the mind of the geologist, that he remarked to my friend "that were he living in Canada, he would not leave a stone unturned until he could secure a right to work the quarry."

"Now," continued B., "I am living in Milwaukee, and engaged in business there, so I can't attend to it, but if you will undertake to secure the location from the government and the Indians, I will pay all your expenses, and furthermore, will send you a map and trace upon it every step necessary for you to take as a guide to find it. What say you, will you try it?"

"I have no particular objection," I replied, "but I think the difficulties will be hard to overcome. First you have to deal with the government, then with the Indians, and last, though not least, the missionary fathers (S. J.), who regard with a jealous eye the welfare of the Indians, and prevent as much as possible the contamination of the white man in their settlements."

"Very true," my friend replied, "but your knowledge of the country, and the people you have to deal with, places you in a position as favorable to succeed as any other person.   In short, nothing ventured, nothing won, is my motto."

With this logic I consented to go.   I was instructed by my friend, on reaching Collingwood to prepare for the expedition a steel drill (an inch bar about four feet long, sharpened and tempered), a mason's hammer, a shovel, two pounds of blasting powder, fuse, etc.   It is needless to say that in the course of six or eight days, my friend complied with his promise promptly and liberally, and a very short time after, I started on my voyage of discovery.   Took the Great Western Railroad at Windsor to Toronto, and reached Collingwood via the Northern Railroad got my supplies, and took passage on the steamer bound for the Sault Ste. Marie, and landed at Killarney, at the head of the Georgian Bay, near the foot of the Lacloche Mountains, some twenty miles distant from the Manitoulin Island.

Hunted up Charles Lamarandier, Indian trader and mail carrier, and worked my passage in his birch canoe, and reached Wickwimikong village, on the Great Manitoulin Island. As the inhabitants were all Indians or half-breeds, there was no place for a stranger to lodge, and it being twelve, midnight, I was advised by the trader to ask for lodgings at the mission house. Leaving him to sleep or pass the night in his canoe, I ascended a rocky faced hill some one or two hundred feet in height, and found the church and mission house adjoining it, built near its edge and commanding a charming view of the bay and country for miles around. A loud knock at the door soon after was answered by a lay brother, who opened it, and upon being informed who I was, provided me with a comfortable bed.

At five o'clock that morning I was disturbed by the same brother with a gentle knock at the door and the usual salutation of the house: "Benedicamus Domino" (praise the Lord). "Who is there?" I replied, instead of "Deo Gratias" (the proper answer) "thanks be to God," and he passed on, satisfied that I was alive, for when the answer is not promptly made, an entrance to the chamber has occasionally disclosed the fact of sudden death or helpless illness.

At that time five of the fathers, viz: Kohler (the superior), Chone, Blatner, Ferrar and Hanepeau, were at the mission house, assisted by four lay brothers. The latter attended to the labours of the farm and indoor work (no women being employed by the Jesuits as house servants), but in harvest and pressing times the fathers gave a helping hand. The same brother who let me in, invited me to take breakfast, and directed me to the dining-room, telling me that I would find a coffee pot, containing three gallons, kept hot on the kitchen stove, and the table supplied with bread and butter, and bowls with maple sugar; all that constituted their breakfast.

After this repast, which the fathers took standing, and in silence (as no conversation is observed at meals, but passages from the lives of the saints or other religious books are read by one of the lay brothers), Father Hanepeau enquired of me "what was my errand?" I then frankly told him all about it, and asked him if I had their consent, as well as the Indians, to prosecute the search. He gave me every encouragement, and said he would assist me in procuring a faithful guide, a birch canoe of his own, a bag of flour twenty-five pounds, a piece of pork fifteen pounds, one pound of tea, a tin kettle, cups, knives, baking powder and salt, maple sugar, a trolling line and spoon hook, for which I paid him. Collecting these together with my drill, shovel and hammer, and tying them in a bundle with my plaid shawl, which was to serve me as a blanket, it was quite equal to one man's pack (about forty pounds), which I would have to carry across two portages. We soon found Pierre Lafrance, a half-breed, the guide, a smart, active and intelligent fellow, who spoke French, of course, broken English, and Indian. Struck a bargain with him, and found him ripe for the occasion. Bidding the father adieu, and thanking him for his trouble and kindness, we struck a path for Manitowoning Bay via Bayfield Inlet. Pierre, with the canoe upside down over his head and shoulders, and I with the pack on my back, crossed the portage, about five miles, in two hours, and struck the inlet, launched our canoe, took off our boots, and paddled for the head of the bay, some

fifteen or twenty miles distant, and from which point to
South Bay, another portage of four or five miles was to be
made. About one p. m., after three hours coasting, Pierre
said we must land and have dinner. These hungry chaps
would eat twenty times a day if you would give it to them,
and I was curious to see him prepare for it; with an axe
which he carried he soon collected along shore plenty of
dry wood, and soon had a brisk fire, then going to the
shore, took from the water a clean flat stone the size of a
soup plate, and stuck it up on edge before the fire to heat,
and seizing the bag of flour, turned down the mouth of it
even with the flour, scooped a hole in it, threw in a pinch
of salt and baking powder, and a cupful of water, and
worked a lump of dough the size of his two fists, flattened
it out on the stone, and again set it before the fire, hung
the tin kettle up over the fire, filled with water, cut three or
four slices of pork and chucked them into the boiling water
for about five minutes, then held my shovel over the fire
and fried the pork, threw in half a cup of tea and one cup
of maple sugar into the kettle, and served the dinner on
pieces of birch bark. Whether it was the exercise, or the

bracing air, or both combined, which hungered me, I know not, but I never partook of food with greater relish. All that was to be cleaned after this repast was the shovel, which Pierre did, by jabbing it into the sand. Great Scott, I thought, if my lady friends would take a leaf from Pierre, what a deal of bother there would be saved, to be sure.

Again we took to our canoe, and with our trolling line caught six black bass. Arrived at the head of Manitowoning Bay at seven p. m., and slept under our canoe, tantalized by fleas inside of our clothing, and devoured by mosquitoes outside. Spent a horrible night, but Pierre swore he never slept better. At daylight we commenced to cross the portage of four or five miles, with the woods on fire, and with great difficulty, climbing over burning trees obstructing our path, arriving at South Bay about nine a. m., and had breakfast, with the addition of black bass.

Launched our canoe and coasted along the barren and bleak shore, with my map as a guide, and on the bright lookout for the object in view, which made its appearance some six or seven miles off, and with striking effect. On landing, I found it unnecessary to resort to blasting, as any quantity of different specimens could be broken off from the layers. Secured them, and prepared to return home, but my first object was to get rid of the fleas, which still tormented me; so, jumping into the canoe, I landed on a solitary rock, stripped myself of every vestige of clothing, spread it in the bright sun, and took a good bath, resulting to my entire satisfaction. After carefully examining and taking soundings at the entrance of the bay, and satisfied of its safe navigation to Lake Huron, I returned to camp and found Pierre in good humor, with a supply of green corn, potatoes and a male white fish just caught, which he obtained from an old Indian. I asked him how he intended cooking it, and if he was going to fry it on my shovel. "Oh, no, spoil," he said; "I show you." So, cutting a stout switch the size of his forefinger, twice the length of the fish, sharpened it at both ends and ran the small end of it through its mouth, nearly to the tail, then stuck it firmly into the sand, before a bright fire, when one side was cooked, turned the other, and when the drip from the mouth fell clear the fish was done, and served on a piece of clean birch bark. Epicures rave about snipe and woodcock served on toast, but give me a whitefish cooked in this way and served on birch bark. But mind, it must be a male fish. Getting ready to start for home, and a favorable breeze springing up, Pierre suggested that we should sail instead of paddling and working so hard. "Where are your sails?" I said. "Monsieur, votre chale est tout ce qu'ille faut" (your shawl is all we want), and giving him my consent to use it, we put ashore, and in about twenty minutes cut two cedar saplings, used my shawl as a sail, and away we scudded at the rate of about six miles an hour. As necessity is the mother of invention, I was fully impressed with the belief that of all garments invented by man (or woman) the shawl is the most useful. Towards night, approaching our camping ground at the head of the bay, the wind had increased to a living gale, when Pierre directed my attention to a bright light on land some distance off, with the simple remark, "Big fire," which it proved to be, for in an incredibly short time it was abreast of us, moving with the whirlwind, and the roar and flashing of a thunder storm. Old patriarchs of the forest, with extended arms aflame and yielding to the tempest's blast, would rock to and fro for a moment and suddenly fall and disappear in the devouring element with the noise of thunder; anon the screeching night owl, or the startled and bewildered wood grouse (partridge), would be seen darting through the fire-lit clouds and suddenly disappear.

Fortunately our camping ground was out of its course, and safely landing, turned our canoe over us on the windward side, and with a good supply of new hay, slept soundly. On my return to Wickwimikong, I found the late Bishop Farrel of Hamilton there, who was on a tour of his diocese, and whose present mission was to confirm some fifty or one hundred Indian children, and I can scarcely express my surprise at the enthusiasm and respect shown to this venerable dignitary, when on his departure from the mission house, he was escorted to Killarney by the chiefs and Indians in their canoes, with all the pomp and ceremony due to royalty itself. On the day following, when ready to start for home, Father Blatner, a Swiss, I think, and a most learned and accomplished linguist (since appointed to a professor's chair at Fordham, N. Y.), approached and enquired how I had succeeded in my search for stone?

After giving him full particulars, he remarked, "I think there is something far more attractive and lucrative on the island, and that is oil." At this startling revelation I pricked up my ears and eagerly desired further information. He then told me that he would, in company with the principal chiefs of the island, accompany me across the bay and I could judge for myself. At the appointed hour we started and arrived at the desired spot, and as we approached it, discovered for several yards around it a perfect calm, and a peculiar colour reflected by the rays of the sun on the water, indicating the presence of the much sought for treasure, and for further proof, on landing the Indians spread a blanket over the water, and after several attempts wrung from it a sufficient quantity to fill a quart bottle. Thus did I strike oil.

Returning to the mission house, the approval of the principal Indians and the missionaries was secured, and the lease afterwards confirmed by the government of 75,000 acres of that portion of the island not ceded, for the explo-

ration and testing of the territory including the whole of
Cape Smith.   I could not leave this interesting spot without expressing my sincere thanks to these friendly Indians
and missionaries for their hospitality, and the confidence
they reposed in me, a perfect stranger; and how often and
with what deep interest have I reflected since, upon the
incidents of my first visit to their establishment.   How men
of such cultured minds, varied talents, nursed and schooled
in the lap of luxury as many of these missionaries are, and
suddenly plunged into this rude, uncultivated, uncivilized
and inhospitable region, with no associates save the untutored children of the forest, is difficult to understand.   It
is not surely for filthy lucre, for that the poor savage does
not possess.   Then what is it?   It must be the anchor of
faith, hope and charity alone!   During my short stay,
Father Hanepeau, the one who procured me a guide,
invited me into his room, where he had a printing press,
and where he taught his young Indian pupils how to print
in the Indian language their hymn books.

Seeing no bed in the room, I said: "Father, where do
you sleep?" "There," he replied, pointing to a shelf with

a buffalo robe to lie on, and another rolled up for a pillow. He was then seventy years old, and for six months in the year spent them in visiting the different encampments for hundreds of miles around, often obliged to draw his toboggan and his traps in winter over two and four feet of snow, on his snow shoes. "How do you celebrate mass in these camps?" I enquired. "This is all I carry on my toboggan or in my canoe," he answered, pointing to a box about four feet long, two feet wide, and eight inches deep; "when I open it in camp it stands on four legs, and when it is empty it serves as my altar. My vestments, chalice, candlesticks, crucifix, etc., are packed in it." "What about your provisions?" I enquired. "Where an Indian can live, so can I," he answered, "dried fish and Indian corn boiled together is breakfast, dinner, and supper." "Pretty tough?" I queried. "Yes, for those who live to eat. I eat to live." I asked no more questions. I dreamed that night I met this old and weatherbeaten pilot of the cross in a gorge of the Lacloche Mountains, just twenty miles distant, and in sight from where I slept, and as the first rays of the morning sun gilded their hoary peaks and the vault of heaven, his only chapel, I heard the tinkling bell of the lonely savage (his only guide and companion), as with head bowed down, on bended knees he announced the elevation of the host. And I beheld the silver-haired and bare-headed pilot in purple chasuble, with arms uplifted and pointing heavenward, and in his fingers were held the offspring of Mary, the Lamb of God, who taketh away the sins of the world, as he implored our Heavenly Father, that through the love, suffering and thorn-crowned agony of this, his dearly beloved Son, in whom he was so well pleased, his wrath against fallen man would be appeased, and the ten thousand angels that were present at the nativity, with the star illuminating the manger in Bethlehem one thousand eight hundred and ninety-two years ago, and the same shepherds then tending their flocks, and the three wise men from the East enthroned on their snow white camels, burdened with their offerings of gold, myrrh, and enveloped in clouds of incense, exclaimed in one voice, "Hosannah, Glory to God in the highest, and on earth peace, good will to men." And the chorus of these angels, shepherds and wise men, added to the savages and pilots, reverberated throughout these mountains of Lacloche, and the awful detonation awoke me in fear and trembling.

The solicitude for the more destitute of the inhabitants of the village is worthy of note. In the basement of this mission house a large room is set apart for their special use, rough benches are placed around it, and in the center a table, and as you enter the outside door, a bell pull is conspicuous, and upon ringing this bell a slide window opens to the kitchen, through which is passed by a lay brother a pan of milk, a loaf of bread, tin cups and spoons. It was seldom the room was without occupants, either with poor squaws and squalid children or old, decrepit men. No charge. For what could these poor creatures offer in return, unless it were a dish of strawberries or huckleberries plucked from the hillside by the squaws and children, or maybe the first whitefish or trout snared in the gill-net of the crippled Indian? In witnessing this scene, how sensibly is one reminded of that beautiful passage, "Simeon Peter, lovest thou me? Yea, Lord, thou knowest that I love thee! Feed my sheep. Feed my lambs!" This precaution is taken to save time and unnecessary intrusion in other parts of the house, as their poverty engenders filth and vermin, and is to be avoided by keeping them at arm's length. Nor are the more thrifty children of both sexes neglected. A school is established close to the mission house, where the boys are taught by the lay brothers of the order in the most necessary branches of education, such as English, French, and geography, simple rules in arithmetic, writing, etc. At a future time I had frequent occasion to visit this school, and was much interested in studying the character of these wild children of the lakes and forests. In reply to my question, are they apt scholars? their old teacher replies: "Yes, very." They are extremely sensitive, however, and require mild and persuasive treatment. Instead of the rod when they deserve it, we imprison them in the school room as their greatest punishment. Such is their innate nature, that like the young duckling which runs to water ere it is full fledged, or the quail or partridge to cover; so does the Indian love to come and go with perfect freedom. For the girls, there is also established an admirable school by a sisterhood of

charity from Cleveland, O., who conduct a small farm connected with their establishment, and attend to all the manual
labors of it. Nay, build their own houses, and are most successful in all branches of refined husbandry. Their example in this line, apart from education, is of incalculable
worth to the natives. In studying the Indian character
one cannot but admire the skill and readiness of both men
and women to acquire and perform mechanical labour in
its various and useful branches. With the assistance of a
head mason and carpenter, they have built a stone church
and mission house, with altar, pews, and windows, displaying as much taste and craft as their more fortunate white
brethren. Where they display their greatest ingenuity and
skill, however, is in the construction of their birch bark
canoes and Mackinaw boats, unrivaled in their safe, buoy-
ant, and sailing qualities. I took the steamer at Killarney
in due time, and arrived at Sandwich, and made no delay
in showing my specimens of stone and oil in Detroit. The
former was pronounced of too flinty a nature to be easily
worked, but Professor Duffield certified to the superior
quality of the oil, after being thoroughly tested, pronounc-

ing it equal to the best Pennsylvania oil; I hastened to Milwaukee to meet B. and report, who when I met him, eagerly inquired, "How about the stone-quarry?" "A failure, I'm afraid," I replied, "but I have struck oil," and producing the bottle gave him its history. Surprised at the sudden turn of affairs, he immediately proposed forming a company, and I was to proceed at once to Quebec, then the seat of government, to ratify our proceedings. A company was formed and $50,000 paid in, and after two years of hard labor sinking six wells from twenty to three hundred and sixty feet deep, purchasing machinery and employing the Indians in the construction of houses, building a dock, chopping cordwood, etc., we only succeeded in producing one hundred barrels of refined oil, pronounced by Parsons, the refiner in Toronto, as the best in Canada, but which exhausted our means, and forced us to abandon the enterprise. In throwing these crude and hastily written reminiscences together, to those who feel interested in the subject it may prove interesting to learn the actual state of things as noted below in the present day. I found the Indians in 1864 scattered over their reservation, but princi-

pally in and about their village (Wickwimikong), and occupying miserable log huts and destitute of every comfort in
their surroundings.   Indeed, after planting their small
patches of corn and potatoes in the spring, they abandoned
their houses, leaving the squaws and children to tend to
their crops until the fall, to gain a precarious living by fishing and hunting in the regions of the Georgian Bay and
Lakes Huron and Superior country.   Impressed with the
idea of their poverty and discomfort, I felt a strong desire
to know how they progressed, not having seen or heard
from them since then, and I had the temerity to write to the
missionaries and requesting the information I so much
desired.   To my agreeable surprise I received a prompt
answer from the superior, Rev. F. J. Hebert, dated October
15, 1891, from which I take the liberty of making the following extract: "The fathers mentioned in your letter have
all passed away.   We number seven priests and seven lay
brothers (it must be borne in mind that this mission em-
braces the Lake Superior region, to Fort William, and this
is their headquarters).   The population of the Indians is
860; many of them are living in comfortable and commo-

dious houses, with carpeted floors, musical instruments and gardens well stocked with fruit trees.

They have progressed rapidly in farming, raising wheat, oats, potatoes, etc., have fine horses and cattle, an industrial school with fifty pupils in regular attendance, where they are taught shoemaking, blacksmithing, tailoring, etc., partly supported by the Canadian Government. Many of them are excellent mechanics, such as masons, plasterers, house builders, etc. A temperance society has been established within the last year and now numbers ninety-six members. They have a large convent, which is at the same time an industrial school with fifty pupils, besides regular boarders. Two large general stores are doing a thriving business, also a saw mill and door and sash factory." The Rev. Father concludes his interesting letter with the humorous remark: "They are not all saints, but I believe they can compare favorably with their more favored white brethren." It is gratifying to learn at all events, that the labours of these isolated missionaries have not been fruitless, and are in profound sympathy as expressed in Pope's beautiful lines:

"Lo the poor Indian whose untutored mind,
Sees God in clouds, or hears him in the wind."

In the summer of 1866 (I think it was) I happened to
be in the village of Killarney, on the Georgian Bay, when
the late Lieutenant-Governor of Ontario, Sir Alexander
Campbell, landed there with the Hudson Bay Company's
bark canoe, and Factor King, of Michipicotons post, with
twenty voyageurs in command, on his return from Lake
Superior, and on his way to the city of Ottawa via that river
and after leaving Killarney landed at the first portage late
in the evening. At early dawn the next morning Sir Alexander arose and though quite lame, with the aid of a cane took
the path for a short walk while breakfast was getting ready,
and had proceeded but a short distance when he descried the
curling smoke from a camp fire, and approaching it, to his
surprise observed a priest in his vestments saying mass, with
his two Indian guides serving him, directly in the path; waiting for a short time until he had finished, he approached and
introduced himself to the priest (Father Hanepeau), to whom
he gave a pressing invitation to return with him to breakfast, which the father modestly declined. Observing a pot

on the fire with a mixture of fish and Indian corn, and three tin pans placed upon the ground, with as many miquens (an Indian wooden spoon) to serve it, "At least," remarked Sir Alexander, "allow me to send you something to diversify your fare." "My guides, no doubt," he replied, "would be glad to receive it, but when that gives out we'll have to fall back on our usual dish." "You have chosen a rough path to follow heavenward," Mr. Campbell remarked. "To you, perhaps, it appears so," replied the priest, "yet I never find my burden too heavy to carry; and we get used to it, like everything else; as the galled shoulder on the plough-horse burns when raw, at first, yet in time it gets callous and ceases to pain." It is needless to say that one of the guides returned with Sir Alexander to his camp, who supplied him with a generous basket of provisions to return with.

THRILLING EXPERIENCE WITH AN INDIAN PILOT.

While prosecuting our search for coal oil at Cape Smith, on the great Manitoulin Island, it became the duty of one of our officers to proceed to Killarney, (the steamboat landing), eighteen miles distant, and receive some thousand feet or more of two-inch iron pipe and have the same transported in open boat to the cape.

The gentleman in question, whom I shall call B., was not long in finding the owner of a large built Mackina boat, a tall athletic Indian by name Joe Miconce, (Bear), who, with his brother, was engaged to make the trip, our friend B. to accompany them and give directions.

The owner of the boat was of the quiet order of Indians, who seldom speak unless there be absolute necessity for conversation.   He was rather a fine looking specimen of the red man in physique and intelligence, although he appeared sullen and his expression of countenance was not altogether pleasing.   He managed his boat well, however, and after a smart trip with a fair wind the party landed at Killarney, and under the order of B., Miconce and his brother proceeded to put on board the iron pipe, while B. went to the office of the freight agent to attend to some other engagement in regard to shipping.

It was about five o'clock in the afternoon when B. returned to the Mackinaw boat and he was somewhat alarmed to find that she was loaded to within six inches of the gunwale. The Indians did not seem to be at all uneasy in the matter, however, and having by much experience witnessed the extraordinary skill and nerve of the Manitoulin Indian and half-breed in the management of the canoe and Mackinaw boat, our friend sought comfort in the easy manner of the two Indians, and got on board.

As the craft was making her first tack off the point at Killarney our friend noticed for the first time that the weather was rough outside and that even where they were the wind blew almost a gale. About this time B. also observed that Miconce was intoxicated and was acting in a very strange manner. In the first place he left his tiller and stern sheets to the care of his brother and our friend B., and reaching through a porthole in the bow of the boat produced a tin gallon canteen and took a good swig of its contents, handed the same to his brother, who followed suit, then repeated the first attack, set his canteen down, scowled at our friend, coiled himself up in a ball and went to sleep.

The wind was increasing from the northwest, the craft was taking in considerable water, which our friend was obliged to bale out the best he could, for the Indian alongside him was becoming too drunk to realize the situation or care for the boat, and after rolling around he, too, slipped down in the boat, and left our friend to its sole management. To haul in sail was a matter attended with considerable danger and exertion, but our friend, being somewhat of a land lubber, and afraid to handle the boat in such a gale, made up his mind that he was much safer with the sails down (which in all probability under these circumstances he was). The boat tossed about in the gale and waves, while our friend sat watching and waiting for the Indians to awake and proceed with the journey.

They had made but about half of the distance of the trip when his position flashed upon his mind, that, with the heavy gale and four tons of iron in an open boat, with two useless Indians, a single gust of wind or wave to swamp it, his situation was a serious one.

As these thoughts passed in rapid succession through his mind B. determined to take the liquor, if possible, from the Indians while they slept and throw it overboard. Our friend B. was of large build, athletic, courageous and was very handy with his fists. As he was about to carry out his intentions in regard to the canteen, Miconce awoke and glared at him with sullen countenance and bleared eyes. He again beckoned to his brother, and reached down for his canteen. This was too much for our friend, who threw off his coat, sprang upon Miconce, and seizing him by the collar of his coat with the left hand and catching hold of his canteen with the right turned it suddenly upside down and the stopper being out the contents in an instant were in the lake.

The struggle to empty the whiskey (for such it proved to be) lasted but an instant, after which Miconce jumped to his feet and, drawing a long clasp knife, made a pass at B., which almost reached him. Before the Indian could recover for another pass our friend, throwing his weight with a well directed blow, caught him under the chin and he fell like a log. The brother then came at B. with a short bar of iron, but he met his match, for another punch sent him sprawling beside the other Indian. Our friend then reached over for the knife, but Miconce, who had recovered from the blow, fought desperately, and in the scuffle a vein in the Indian's left wrist was laid open and the boat was bespattered with blood. The Indian's frantic exertions, yells and execrations became somewhat modified by the loss of blood and bursting into a loud whoop he was seized with an hysterical fit fell in the bottom of the boat, where he soon slept soundly alongside his brother, who lay there half conscious, but not caring to renew the fight. Our friend then took his white pocket handkerchief, tore it into strips, bound up the bleeding wrist of Miconce, and signalling a passing fishing smack left the two Indians to the mercy of the storm, which was still at its height. He arrived at the cape safe and sound and gave his experience to the missionaries, who had, by the way, recommended Joe Miconce to him as a reliable man. The following morning Miconce and his brother arrived at their destination with their iron pipe in good order, quite sober and humble, and after having his wrist dressed by one of the missionaries, who took occasion to give him a good dressing at the same time, sought out our friend B. and humbly asked his forgiveness, which was granted.

But, sad to relate, these poor fellows the following year were caught in a gale of wind off Bear's Rump Island with their boat loaded with gravel, when the boat swamped and they never were seen or heard of afterwards. Too much fire water again.

THE BOOK PEDDLER.

On the 18th of June, 1869, the anniversary of the battle of Waterloo—the day on which the fate of Europe
was sealed by the Iron Duke placing his iron heel on
the neck of Napoleon the Great, from which it was not
released until death, on St. Helena's barren isle, put an
end to his eventful career—I found myself sauntering
down Main street in the City of Milwaukee, dejected in
spirit and absorbed with the troubles that then over-
whelmed me.   Suddenly and unexpectedly thrown out of
employment by the removal from the city of my generous employer, I bent my steps to the Young Men's Library, of which I was an honorary member; and here "I
will pause to remark" that I know of no institution that
I have yet seen that will compare with it for its admirable arrangement, the collection of its library, and the
courteous and gentlemanly deportment of its attendants.
Entering this seat of learning I seized the first volume
within reach, threw myself into a capacious arm chair,

and was soon lost in following the drift of that illumined and exalted mind, "Fenelon," when a gentleman of quiet and pleasing address approached me and thus introduced himself:

"Your name is B., is it not?" To this rather unexpected question I nodded assent, whereupon the stranger continued: "Your friend, the librarian, has recommended you to me as a fit person to canvass this city for the most attractive book of the times, viz: 'Lossing's Life of George Washington,' illustrated; my name is J. Rogers, of the firm of Rogers Bros., Lake street, Chicago, book publishers, and if you feel inclined to accept the job, say so." Taken rather by surprise, with the idea flashing across my mind that I was about as fit for a bookseller as the man in the moon, I replied to Mr. Rogers that I would think about the matter and let him know on the morrow at his room, 20 East Water street, Kirby House. Agreeably to appointment, the next day I found Mr. R. and told him I would accept his offer; he thereupon instructed and directed me in my duties, which were:

First—On his return to Chicago he was to send by return steamer a certain number of volumes one, two and three, in different styles of binding—No. 1, gilt morocco; No. 2 calf, and No. 3, cloth—to be sold at $4, $3, and $2 respectively.

Second—To be careful in getting reliable subscribers, for in that depended our success of course.

Third—Never to expose the prospectus (sample book), for folks generally had an aversion to book peddlers.

Now, how in "Sam Hill" was I to sell a book "like a pig in a poke," without exposing it, puzzled me. Still, it was my duty to obey instructions no matter what happened, consequently I had suitable cords or pieces of braid attached inside of my coat which afforded a means for carrying the prospectus unobserved. Thus schooled and armed with my prospectus concealed in the breast of my coat, I made my exit on Main street. "What," I reasoned with myself on reaching the pavement, "has it come to this? I, the descendant of an honored name, reduced to this strait?" Sad and crushing thought. Then came the counter reflection: "Is it honest; is there any position, occupation or service that man is called upon to fulfill that we should find fault with or repine at? Perish forever the craven thought! Let man aspire to higher aim. In God is our trust, and we'll never submission to His will refuse." Thus moralizing, I started for the first ward. This was generally occupied by laborers and mechanics. It was my impression that I could face people of that class on more equal grounds than the elite, in my first lessons. Approaching a shoemaker's shop I found the door wide open. A sign, representing a large boot, on which had been artistically painted the name of the proprietor and sole occupant of the building, Patrick O'Flaherty, adorned the top of the doorway. The noise produced by the shoemaker's hammer and lap-stone in pounding a piece of sole leather seemed to drown and absorb everything else. On approaching the industrious proprietor I inquired, "Would you be kind enough to make me a pair of shoe thongs?" "Certainly," he replied, and bade me take a seat on a comfortable leather-covered shoemaker's bench in front of him. Seizing his cutting board and throwing it across his lap he picked up a piece of calfskin, drove his awl through the center of it, then trimmed the leather until it assumed the form of a perfect circle, withdrew the awl, imbedded his knife firmly in the board, made a slit in the leather the width of the lace or string desired, placed his left thumb nail at a proper distance from the knife to serve as a guage, seized the end of the leather with his right hand, gave it a quick jerk, and, in the twinkling of an eye sput out a yard of it; he then rolled it upon his board, blackened it and handed to me. "What have I to pay you," I asked. "Five cints, yer honor." On handing him the change I observed that the way he pronounced that coin would lead a person to believe that he came from the "ould sod." "Yis, indade, and shure the way ye deteckted me ye must kum frum the same." "The best half of me on my mother's side did," I replied, "but I have become so galvanized with the people surrounding me that I am fast losing my nationality." "Faith, thin, I cud well belave ye; I feel the same myself," rejoined O'Flaherty, as he scrutinizingly surveyed me from head to foot. "Still this is a great country," I said. "The gratest in the wurrld," was the response. "And Washington was the greatest man and soldier in it," said I. "That's true for ye," was the quick reply of my new acquaintance, who began to evince a disposition to be sociable and talkative. "Was he an Irishman?" I asked. This question rather puzzled the thrifty cobbler. After pondering over it carefully for a few moments in a vain endeavor to give a correct answer, he inquiringly remarked, "Wasn't Wellington?" "I'm not so sure about that, but I'll see." This afforded me an excellent opportunity to exhibit my prospectus, which was quickly removed from its hiding-place and opened in such a manner as to attract attention. I then took great pains in showing Washington's Virginia home, his house, furniture, boots, etc. "That's a moighty foine book ye hev there," exclaimed O'Flaherty, as he glanced at the prospectus with its elaborate binding. "Yes, indeed," I replied, "next to the bible the finest book printed." "Where did ye get it?" he asked. "Where there are plenty more," said I. "Is it cha-a-pe?" he inquired. "That depends on the quality—$4, $3 and $2," I rejoined. "Faith'n I think I'll tak the $2 one," said he. "All right," I replied, "you shall have one to-mor-

row morning. Put your name down." "I can't write," he
said, "you put it down fur me." This I gladly did and
bade Mr. O'Flaherty good morning, who, on accompanying me to the door, loudly exclaimed "Long loife to yer
honor." On hearing this I said to myself, "if Pat only
knew I was making a dollar out of him he would have
wished me to the devil instead." After leaving Mr.
O'Flaherty's establishment I visited a baker's shop, the
proprietor of which, Jules Vantrampe, as his name
implies, was a Dutchman. On entering the door
an awful clatter caused by a bell suspended by means
of a steel spring over the doorway greeted my ears, which
also aroused Jules, who was busily engaged at a bread
trough in the back room at the time. Vantrampe quickly
made his appearance wearing upon his head a square-top
paper cap, while a sheet or table cloth reaching from his
jaws to his toes covered his person. His sleeves were
tucked up to the elbow, displaying a pair of well-formed
hands and arms which were partially covered with flour
or dough. Huge drops of sweat were coursing down his
red chops and he was looking about as savage as a meat

axe. I mildly informed him that I had a valuable book I would like to show him. This chap apparently did not believe in fooling away his time with a book-peddler, for he gruffly replied, "Nix furstand Henglish," at the same time slamming the door in my face. This rebuff served to whet my appetite, to appease which, it being near noon-time, I wended my way to Best's lager beer saloon. Best made his own beer and in addition ran the largest saloon in the place, the magnitude and splendor of which was quite surprising. Twenty-five or thirty tables covered the floor at which were usually seated four persons. I approached the bar as near as I could, seated myself, rapped upon the table and called for a schuper of beer, a pretzel and a piece of limburger cheese. The landlord waited upon me. I asked him, as a stranger, to join me in a glass, to which he raised no objection, but quickly got his glass and sat down beside me. "If I'm not mistaken you are fond of literature," I ventured to remark after clearing my throat by a good draught of refreshing and exhilarating beer. "Very," he replied, "but my time is so engrossed with beer that the brain is sadly neglected." "Very likely you have grown up sons and daughters," I continued, "who are of your turn of mind. I have an excellent book, and it will surprise me greatly if you do not pronounce it a work that no true American should be without." "What is it," he inquired. "The greatest work of the age—'Lossing's Life of Washington, illustrated,'" I rejoined, at the same time producing the prospectus. The superb binding immediately caught his eye and he subscribed for a $4 edition. We drank to the health of Bismarck, and as I was about to leave he said: "When you first came in I took you for a German, and you may think yourself very much flattered when I tell you if I met you five times a day I would be forcibly reminded of Kaiser William." We then drank a bumper to Kaiser William's health, whereupon I thanked Best for the compliment, promising at the same time to return the following day with the book. This sale led to our taking many schupers together afterwards. Somewhat elated at my success I sauntered forth to new fields. After walking a short distance I approached a respectable looking residence on the same street and rang the door bell. In

response to my ring the door was partially opened by
the maid of all work, slip shod, who, with a napkin round
her head, snappishly yelled, "What do you want?"   "I
would like to show the lady a very fine book," was my
polite reply. "Misses told me never to let a book-man
enter the house; if I did she would discharge me," saying which she closed the door, which closed the scene. I
then returned to Main street, one of the most fashionable streets of the city, and entered a large millinery establishment, whose plate glass windows filled with bon-
nets, caps, ribbons, and corsets attracted my attention.
Here I found a half dozen girls operating their tread-mills
and kicking up an awful racket. An elderly lady occupied a prominent seat overlooking the 'fry.' On approaching the girls I asked if Miss Cinderella Tompkins (ficti-
tious, of course), was within.   The girls stopped their
tread-mills, looked at each other and giggled. The old
hen of this full-fledged brood, looking over the upper
rim of her gold specks, said, "There's no ·such person
here." "I am exceedingly sorry for that," I replied, "she
is a lady of my acquaintance, and being an expert needle-

woman I thought it likely she would be engaged in this, the most fashionable establishment in the city." Gracefully bowing to her I was about to depart when she asked me if there was anything in her line that I wanted. "No," I replied, "but there may be something in mine that would exceedingly interest you as well as these industrious young ladies." She asked me what it was, and drawing forth my Prospectus, I exposed it to their delighted gaze. The old lady took a $4 volume, and two of the girls a $2 volume, remarking at the same time that they could not pay immediately. "Oh, that makes not the slightest difference," I said, "in a month will do." Thanking them for their kindness I bade them adieu. On the whole I could not complain of my canvass. I found it more successful, however, with the laboring classes, and for that reason made it my aim to watch for the time of their leisure hours, particularly at noon, when they could be seen by the hundreds at their different factories. This class of people I found far more eager to read than I dreamed of. I had attended one of these factories some distance from the heart of the city, and on my return homeward was struck with the appearance of a mansion quite out of the way of ordinary buildings in point of architectural design and in the tasteful ornamentation of the grounds surrounding it, in fact denoting the residence of a millionaire, or hog, corn, or beef speculator, or, perhaps, a railroad magnate, or banker. To tackle this place required brass, strategy, and considerable self possession, otherwise it would be a deplorable and mortifying failure. Arousing my spirits with the old proverb, "nothing ventured nothing won," I opened the gate and found myself on a neatly-kept, wide, gravelly walk leading to the marble steps of the mansion. On either side of this walk were beds of choicest flowers whose delicious odor filled the air. Two whirligig fountains in full play, one on each side, cast their beautiful silver spray which glistened in the rays of the declining sun. Ascending the steps, a massive mahogany door met my gaze, by the side of which was the usual plated bell-pull. Seizing this I gave it a desperate pull and the sound of the tinkling bell could be heard from cellar to garret. Presently a voice was heard from upstairs saying, "Susanna, go to the door."

The door was opened and I was struck with Susanna's appearance. She was the living image of the bright creole I had often read about. Her dark wavy hair fell in graceful curls over her shoulders, in striking contrast to her white muslin dress, which encircled a form of faultless beauty. Staring in her dark, liquid eyes provoked from her a smile which disclosed her handsome ivory teeth. There is a kind of mesmerism at times, that we cannot account for, which asserts its sway. She seemed to be aware that I was struck with her appearance. I politely inquired if Mr. S—— was at home. She answered, "No, he will not be home from the bank till six in the evening." "Is Mrs. S—— within?" I asked. "Yes," was the reply. "Pray be kind enough to say that a gentleman wishes to see her." "Give me your card," she said. "Oh, never mind the card," I replied, "she'll know who I am before I leave." She then invited me in and led me to the drawing room, very likely taking me for the uncle of her mistress or very intimate friend. I made up my mind that the poor girl made an awful faux pas and would catch it after I was gone for letting me in. On

entering this drawing room I was struck with my noise-
less tread, lost in a thick Turkey carpet. A table occupied each end of the room, while in the center vases of
choicest flowers filled the well ventilated apartment with
delicious fragrance. Scattered about the vases were richly
bound works of latest editions. Commodious arm chairs
invited you to their embrace. Heavy lace curtains drooped
from ceiling to floor. The crimson velvet papered walls
were embellished with choicest works of art both in paint-
ings and engravings. A harp stood in one corner of the
room while at the other end, and in an opposite corner
was a $2,000 Weber grand piano. A guitar, apparently
of great value, occupied a conspicuous place on one of
the finely upholstered sofas. I thought to myself there
must be music in the air. Everything denoted refinement,
culture and taste. Seating myself in an arm chair I was
soon lost in reflection. Five, ten, fifteen, twenty minutes elapsed and yet no word from the lady. Rising
from my chair, assisted in so doing by the elastic spring
cushion, I sauntered to a picture immediately in front of
me. It was a steel engraving, a copy of Claude Lor-

raine's celebrated painting, "Roman Edifices in Ruins." I
was familiar with this chef d'euvre, having had one in my
possession for many years, but which, alas, was unfortunately lost by fire. Huge elm trees occupying the fore-
ground cast their deep shadows over a stream that invited
the thirsty herds to slake their thirst, some of
which were standing in it up to their knees. The
goat herd, a girl tending her stubborn goats,
formed an attractive feature, while in the distance the faintest outlines of the ruined edifices all inspired to fill the soul with admiration for such a scene
and such an art. Lost in reverie in admiring this sub-
lime work I came suddenly to my senses on hearing the
rustling of a moir-antique sweeping the broad and circling
stairway. In a moment after the lady of the house floated
in, as it were, on airy wings, and, with an inconccivably
gracious bow, presented herself, as much as to say, "here
I am, sir, what do you want?" From her appearance I
could tell that she had been carefully studying her dress,
no doubt thinking that I had come to negotiate a loan,
perhaps, of a million dollars or so from her husband to

secure a grip on some wheat, timber or pork transaction. She was very handsome. (I found out afterward she was a young bride.) I felt as if I would sink through the floor for having placed myself in such an awkward and humiliating position.   Folding my arms, and reverently bowing to her, I opened the ball as follows: "Madam, I have a thousand apologies to make to you for this untimely intrusion, but, attracted by this beautiful palace and the charming tout ensemble of its surroundings, I could not resist the temptation of offering to your cultured mind a book which would help to adorn the beautiful collection of works before me, and which would probably to you be a volume the most interesting, 'Lossing's Illustrated Washington,' a history of the father of this great country." With my truthful and earnest gaze I watched her countenance and if she was at all angered it was for a moment and as quickly disappeared. She remarked that of course in subscribing to so valuable a work she would like me to bring it to her for inspection, whereupon the prospectus was immediately withdrawn from its place of concealment. On producing the captivating article she

was quite charmed with its morocco binding and ordered two copies, one for herself and one for her sister
in Green Bay. At this moment the door bell rang and
in bounced her husband, who was rather taken by surprise on beholding a stranger. A red Irish setter was at
his heels, who, on seeing his mistress, flew to claim her
caresses, observing which his master cried out, "Bruno,
to kennel," and to kennel the dog flew like lightning. I
was struck with the gentleman's appearance, in one hand
was his light straw hat and in the other was grasped a
knotty black thorn stick, his auburn curly hair was mat-
ted on his forehead with perspiration; his face had never
been touched with a razor; his well knit frame was clothed
in a light grey summer suit of admirable fit; no gold chain,
finger rings, etc., were to be seen on his person; he seemed
to think that beauty unadorned was adorned the most.
Just the kind of a chap to ride a steeplechase, spring over
a six-foot barred gate, swim the Niagara river or captivate
the Irish beauty near him. The lady, addressing her husband, said: "Arthur, this person brought here a book
for my inspection, and I have bought two volumes from

him." "I am only too glad they please you," he replied. On turning over the cover and seeing my name on the fly-leaf the husband inquired, "Are you from Canada?" "Yes," I replied. "Are you any relation to Charles B., of Sandwich, George and Horace B., of Montreal, or Francois B., of Quebec?" he asked. "They are all brothers or cousins," I replied. "Bless me," continued the gentleman, "they are all my most intimate friends who have always extended me the warmest hospitality. Glad to see you. My wife, Mr. B." I bowed gracefully to her salutation. "Caroline," he added, "I have had a long walk and feel dreadfully oppressed. Order some re-freshments, please." The lady immediately disappeared, and in a few moments returned, accompanied by Susan-na, (the sylph), who carried a silver tray containing a bottle of Cognac, two bottles of sparkling Catawba, and a silver pitcher filled with ice water. "Brandy or Cataw-ba," the gentleman asked. "Brandy I can get any day, Catawba never," I replied; "so I'll take the wine." He drew the cork, which flew like that from a champagne bottle, filled a glass for madam and then requested me to help myself. I generally obey orders and consequently followed his instructions. We saluted each other and imbibed the sparkling and delicious draught. "Oh, Sam Hill," said I to myself in thinking of my prospectus, "what a weapon; thou feedest the hungry, slaketh the thirsty and clothe the naked." The exhilarating glass warmed the banker's Irish heart, and, addressing himself to me, he said, "Mr. B., I crossed the Atlantic in February last and stole from Erin this gem of the dear Emerald Isle and she brought her harp with her. Caroline," he said, looking at his wife, "give us the song you captivated me with on the flowery banks of the Liffy, 'The Harp that Once Thro' Tara's Hall.'" With the most graceful ease she moved to the harp, seated herself, swept with delicate touch the strings of the instrument, and then poured forth her soul in song, as none but a child of Erin can do. The pathos, the melody, the voice; what can I compare to it. Oh, for the pen of a Scott to describe that scene and the pencil of a Raphael to paint it. After expressing the belief that I had been sorely trespassing I bade my host and hostess adieu, leaving them to their reflec-

tions and they to mine to dream of that divinity which
shapes our ends, "rough hew them as we may." On the
following day while in the vicinity of the Menominee
bridge a comical looking sign attracted my attention.
Two whitewash brushes, crossed, were painted over
the doorway, as also the name, "gEorGe WasHinG-
ton, ciTy whIte waShEr." The door stood wide open.
The air was clear and hot, Sol's meridian rays striking
you to the brain if not well guarded. Immediately opposite this rude structure was a large brick school house, in
the cupola of which the bell was striking the hour of
noon, while from its portals belched forth two streams,
one of boys and the other of girls. One of the latter,
about fourteen or fifteen years old, black as ebony and
sprightly as a fawn, made for the door where I had taken
refuge. It was her home. I inquired if the whitewasher
could be seen. She replied, "Pap will be here soon for
his dinner." Presently the father made his appearance.
In one hand he carried a large tin pail while with the
other he firmly held the ten-foot handle of a whitewash
brush which was thrown across his shoulder. His old

white stovepipe hat was battered out of shape and was very much discolored. The black clay pipe which he sported was about three inches in length and turned upside down, and it appeared a matter of perfect indifference whether it was alight or not. His arms were bare to the shoulders. The blue cotton shirt and pants which he wore appeared to have been made in one piece. The heels of his red, lime-burned boots were turned under, compelling him to walk with a kind of halting gait. "Your name is George Washington," I observed as the old man approached me. "So de white folks calls me," was the reply. "And are you from old Virginia?" "Jis-so." "How many years since you left there?" "About forty-two last plantin'." "You come from a very large and distinguished family?" "Can't tell much 'erbout 'em, it's so long, long ago." "Do you think you would know any members of the family if you saw their likeness?" "I mought, and again I moughten't," was the response. "Well, we'll look and see," I said, at the same time drawing forth my prospectus, exposing to the old man and his daughter a view of George and Martha Washington, their Virginia home, etc., whereupon the young fawn exclaimed, "Pap, dem's white folks, des no kin to us." "Hold on," I replied, "they were all black once and after a time turned white. After two or three generation you'll all turn white, too, and be of one family." "Boss, what's dat book woth eny-how," asked the anxious-looking fawn. "The cheapest edition is two dollars," I replied. "We can't pay you for it befo' three months, we am so poo'." said the girl. "Well, then," I said, "I'll make you a present of one. Come with me and get it, for it would be a pity to live without knowing who your ancestors were." It is perhaps need-less to add that the girl followed me and got the book.

Considering my deficiency in brass, self-confidence and strategy my career as a book canvasser was about as suc-cessful as could be expected. There was one thing I learned, to my entire satisfaction, namely, that truly one-half the world knows very little how the other half lives, and if you wish to satisfy yourself on that subject get a book agency from J. Rogers Bros., book publish-ers, Chicago, as I did, and prove it.

VISIT TO THE SAULT STE. MARIE.

A new route to the Sault from Windsor and Detroit was established in the summer of 1894 (by way of the North Channels leading to St. Mary's river, by the steamer Cambria), embracing one of the most attractive, picturesque and charming landscapes on the continent of America—attractive to the lovers of sport by gun or rod, where twenty thousand islands or more afford varied and innumerable opportunities to whip the dark and limpid waters with gaudy fly, or snare the unlucky bass or dore, with killing and treacherous spinning spoon encircling them.

Although familiar with the old route from Collingwood to the Sault by way of Killarney, this new one is different, and I felt not a little interested when I found that the Cambria had commenced to run on it this fall, preparatory to resuming it in the ensuing spring, after undergoing a thorough overhauling this winter.

Stepping on board on the 9th instant, with a party of five, we secured double staterooms, furnished with all the conveniences reasonably required. The hour having arrived to depart, Captain Gidly, in uniform (the very type of a dauntless and brave Acadian sailor), climbs the iron ladder leading to the pilot house, with the agility of a panther, and his ever ready and trustworthy Mate McKay, anxiously waiting for the order, in loud and stentorian voice, cries out, "Let go your headline, haul in your sternline," and the shrill, thrice-sounding whistle is heard, and slowly the Cambria leaves her quiet sleeping berth, and prepares to buffet with the angry waves of Huron's Lake and the turgid waters of the Georgian Bay. Touching at the beautiful City of the Straits (Detroit) for passengers and freight, we bend our course to the Canadian channel and hug the shores of the beautiful Belle Isle, affording us a charming view of its mosque-like buildings, its sinuous canals and flower-decked islets, and passing the tidy little brick lighthouse at the end of the island, steer our course for the lighthouse on Grosse Pointe, flanked on our right by the Isle au Peche (vulgarly called Peach Island), with Hiram Walker's summer villa looming in the distance. We are now fully entered upon the quiet waters of Lake St. Clair, and in full view of

Grosse Pointe proper, which, with marine glass in hand, gives us a commanding view of its millionaire summer retreats, beautified by ornamental trees and shrubs, close-clipped hedges, and clouded with choicest flowers of autumn.   Directly here our attention is claimed by two enormous dredges, employed by the American Government to deepen the channel to twenty-one feet, and gradually we lose sight of them as they plunge their mighty iron clad arms in the watery deep, and, with Herculean sweep deposit their well-filled spoons in the dumping scows.   As we are about to lose sight of land the stalwart, eagle-eyed captain steps down from the pilot house and quietly instructs his wheelsman to steer "north east quarter east," which will bring us to the mouth of the St. Clair Flats Canal.   As we gradually approach its wide and open channel, it appears planted on either side with rows of dwarfed willow trees extending a mile in length, and its entrance guarded by its ever watchful lighthouse.

Emerging from the canal, the spacious and Venetian club houses, hotels and villas come in full view, with striking effect, each varying in design, color and size to suit the caprice of their respective owners, and each one perched upon knolls, dredged from the surrounding flats. As we plow through the swift waters of the St. Clair River, we soon approach Walpole Island, the favorite resort of excursionists, and immediately opposite is Harsen's Island, a fashionable retreat also from summer heat. Here the somber sky shuts out the view, and we retire to our saloon, delighted with our day's experience. Touching at Sarnia during the night, we are well into Lake Huron at seven a. m. on the 10th, enjoy a comfortable breakfast liberally provided by our courteous and gentlemanly purser, Mr. Kelly, and waited upon by civil and attentive waiters. After breakfast we step to the promenade deck, and with field glass survey the Canadian rugged shore, and reach Goderich, whose harbor is formed by a cleft in the high clay bank, through which the River Maitland flows, with lighthouse perched on its summit on the right, and the picturesque residence embowered in dwarfed evergreens on the left, once the residence of the Galt family. Not a great deal can be said of this harbor in its present state, as we found it difficult with our steamer to turn in it, for want of water, but an improved and powerful dredge is at work, with prospects of great results.

Leaving Goderich, we touch at Kincardine and Southampton, then steer for the Isle of Coves, the entrance to the Georgian Bay. The night is dark and tempestuous, and as we leave its lighthouse the Cambria feels the buffets of its chopping seas, but forges on and with steady roll (unpleasant to our lady passengers) doubles Cape Smith at early dawn, and with the village of Wickwimikong looming in the distance at the head of its bay, we soon enter the north channel, and call at Manitowoning, an Indian village on the Great Manitoulin Island. The scenery now assumes an air of grandeur, and as the misty atmosphere clears, the chain of the Lacloche Mountains appears in sight, and as we thread our way through these intricate channels spread at their feet, some of them the size of large lakes (the favorite haunt of the sea gull), we descry one following at a long distance in the wake of our steamer. With measured flap of wing, he approaches within pistol shot, with head inclined and eye intent upon the blue and crystal waters. We throw a morsel of broken cracker in the wake of the steamer, and mark his graceful evolutions. Unlike the bird of prey, who darts like a thunderbolt and pounces on his victim, this white-winged visitor is strikingly different; the crumb has scarcely touched the water, when his eagle eye sees it, he changes at once the flap of wing and extends his broad pinions to full extent, changes his course of flight, and with graceful circling curves descends to the precious morsel, extends his webbed feet, alights with the grace of a dancing nymph, settles upon the ruffled waters, seizes his crumb, and again ascends and pursues his flight, to renew the feat, to the envy of his fellow fleet-wings, who are clamorous to participate in the feast, and rapidly increase in numbers.

We emerge at last into Lake George's devious channel. From this point of view our course would be abruptly stopped at the foot of the mountain, miles distant, but as we near the end of the lake a sudden turn northerly brings us into the St. Mary's River again, flanked on either side by the thriving settlement of Garden River, etc. We soon are in sight of the Sault Ste. Mary's city, and stopping first on the Canadian side, cross over to the American shore, when

our captain receives a message from Mr. Brown, of Port
Arthur (the courteous and gentlemanly manager of our
boat), desiring us to wait for him, as he is on his way down
per steamer Empire. This happens most opportunely for
our party, as it gives us ample time to see both canals. Our
boat lands us near the foot of the canal, and we hasten to
see its wonderful locks, passing on our way the beautiful
public park tastefully laid out with ornamental trees, dark
in foliage, peculiar to this climate, and a fountain in full
play, with a spacious basin catching the falling spray, in
which disport the lively speckled trout. Mounting a flight
of stone steps, we are on a level with the top of the canal,
and immediately opposite the engine house of hydraulic
power, managed by a gentlemanly officer in uniform, who
extends to us every courtesy. A large steam barge loaded
with lumber, with her two consorts, are in the lock, and
presently the lever is turned, the gates from below are
opened, and the torrent of water rushes out with the noise
of thunder. Slowly sinks the imprisoned fleet until the
water level is reached, when they glide gently away. A
new lock is being constructed alongside of the present one,

which is to be of far greater capacity. We visit the large Hotel Iroquois, overlooking the park, and return to the Canadian side by one of the steam ferry boats that ply between the two places. Through the kindness and politeness of Mr. Templeton, the officer of the customs, who kindly offered us his carriage, we were enabled to visit the canal now being constructed on the Canadian side, but could form but an imperfect idea of its construction, owing to the enormous debris with which it is encumbered, but were informed that every effort is being made to complete it next year.

Leaving the Sault on our return at early dawn to thread our way through the intricate passages by daylight, we stop at St. Joseph's Island for supplies of ice, milk, fish and potatoes, the former remarkable for its thickness and purity, and the latter famed for their delicious qualities, and also its maple sugar, with which we supplied ourselves. Our next principal stopping place is at Gore Bay, an inlet of the Great Manitoulin Island, remarkable for the beauty of its entrance, its bluff highland, clothed with dwarf evergreen, hiding the naked rocks from top to the very edge of its dark and deep waters, affording a safe and quiet harbor. Our vigilant and wideawake captain and mate think it proper to remain here, and wait till morning, until the fog lifted, and we then proceeded on our way. Again, on doubling Cape Smith and entering Georgian Bay, we encounter the unquiet ripple of its restless waters, which increase to a stiff breeze, portending a stormy night. So the captain puts in at Tober Mory, formed by nature, one of the most perfect harbors in the world. We leave at daylight and reach Goderich in time to avoid a living gale, which detains us two nights and a day, and are agreeably entertained there by Mr. Ira Lewis and family and friends, and on the 18th arrived at Windsor at five a. m., much pleased with our pleasant trip.

A SKETCH SHOWING, AMONG OTHER THINGS, HOW THE BRUCE MINES IN ALGOMA WERE DISCOVERED.

The peace of Europe, declared after the bloody field of Waterloo in 1818, was the cause of a great reduction in the British army, and hundreds of its officers sought a place of rest in Canada, and among the many was a Capt. D., who, with ample means and a grant from the government of 600 acres of land to which he was entitled for his long and faithful services, settled down in the township of Barrie. He had married an Italian lady of rare and singular accomplishments, highly educated, the mistress of several languages, English, French, Spanish and Italian, the latter denoting the home of her birth, gifted in music, song and poetry, and with all a connoisseur in the culinary art of the most refined English, French and Italian taste. She had been twice a widow before her last marriage, the first of an Italian gentleman, by whom they had no issue, the second of an English clergyman

AN INDIAN BRIDE.

by whom she had two sons, her third marriage was to a distinguished officer in the British army, of blunt, severe and arrogant manner, by whom she had one son. It was the pride and aim of their lives to give these three sons the best education they could in their unsettled and rambling life, with a view of completing their studies in the gay, festive and alluring city of the world, seductive Paris. Consequently they became pronounced linguists and adepts in the knowledge of the finest brands of champagne, mozelle, Hock, Burgundy, etc. Versed in all that pertained to operatic style and song, unapproachable admirers of female beauty, and an ungovernable and recherche taste for the most pronounced epicurean dishes of the times. Added to these so-called accomplishments, the three sons were remarkable in physique and gentlemanly bearing.

The father settled in Canada about the year 1820 and the sons followed about two years after, and such were their accomplishments that, drop them into any portion of the habitable world, they would make their mark.

They were, indeed, the pride and envy of their devoted parents.

The eldest, in making his appearance in Little York in 1822, soon became the lion of the town. Marked attention was paid to him by the ladies, and gentlemen courted him for his polished manners and his versatile and broad knowledge of the world, politically, morally and socially. His thorough knowledge of the French and English languages was a free and easy passport to him in any circle of society. The ordinary pursuits of life, involving application, study and labor, however, were too irksome to him and an annoying restraint upon his various inclinations to shoot, fish, sail, dance, dine and sup, and he secretly fancied a wider field, an unlimited scope in the mountainous districts of Ontario and Algoma, whose mountains, lakes and streams would give him free liberty to enjoy the scope of his inclinations. After a time he became tired of his luxurious life in Little York (now Toronto) and sought the quiet, cozy and comfortable home of his stepfather in the county of Barrie. Here his occupation was indeed a diversified one.

Getting up at five in the morning, cleaning out the cow and horse stables and the pig-pens, and in pressing times helping the milkmaid with her dozen or more cows, chopping and carrying in wood to cook his own breakfast, yoking his oxen and plowing till noon, with an hour for dinner and again at the plow or harrow till six, then supper on mush and milk. Then with the fowls to roost, and repeat the next day the same toil, variegated only to suit the weather and seasons. Now logging the wood piles and firing the brush heaps, again husking the corn in the open field. Then in the fall butchering twelve or fifteen hogs, (scalding himself in the operation), then obliged to rip them open and plunge both hands into the hot entrails, and completing the labor by washing and cleaning thoroughly the carcases for market.

While one day employed in the latter occupation, exhausted, weary and unwashed, a former school-mate in Paris, (St. Martin), fished him out and thus saluted him: "Great Heavens, my friend, this you? Reduced to this situation, far worse than abject slavery. What has brought you to this state of misery?" "Fate," he innocently replied. "Why do you remain here?" continued his school-mate. "Come where I have been! See what I have seen! This continent is ours, unlimited in its prairies and forests, its lakes and streams of crystal waters, teeming with golden-eyed and speckled trout; its vales and mountains, unexplored and filled with untold wealth; its dusky inhabitants free from all care in this transitory world, but to feed on nature's bounteous gifts, their sole occupation to trace the timid deer, to seine with finest thread the warry whitefish and trout in the invisible gill-net, to pluck and gather the luscious huckleberry and the prickly goose and raspberry. The Indian has indeed a fine life, and the dusky squaw, untrammeled with the care of her infant papoose, suspends it under the foliage of the shady maple, to be rocked to sleep by the lullaby of the waving branches and rustling leaves. The life is enchanting, my boy, and unknown to the white man." "Truly, your description is very alluring and worthy of consideration. Gladly would I make the change from this detestable drudgery, but, pray, where is this state of bliss to be found, St. Martin?" "Why," continued St. Martin, "in the charming islands of the Georgian Bay, the straits of the Saint Marie's river and the boundless regions of Lakes Huron and Superior, where the trace of the white man is scarcely known." Then almost in the same breath he asked, "I say, old fellow, I am d—d thirsty after a twenty-mile tramp through the woods. Has the old man anything in his cellar in the way of a glass of old sherry, Hock or St. Julian?" "No," replied the other, "not a drop of anything, but cursed rot-gut Canadian whiskey, fit only to cure the bite of a rattlesnake or cur with the rabies, or kill the botts in the paunch of a horse, but, say, how will a bowl of buttermilk do?" "Well, all right, give me a pull at anything; that's better than water." He then takes his buttermilk with a grin and tells his friend, "I'm off for the Sault Ste. Marie, old chap, and a line from you hereafter would be most acceptable. Farewell, au revoir." In the evening, while sitting around the capacious and glowing wood fire the stepfather noticed his stepson with pipe ablaze in thoughtful mood, and observed to him, "What has ruffled and disturbed you?" "Why, my friend St. Martin has given me such glowing

accounts of the upper lake region, their mineral mountain resources, the abundance of game, fish and fruit, and
withal the ease and comfort of their dusky inhabitants,
that I feel a very strong inclination to test the alluring
bait, with your kind indulgence," replied the son.   "I
would only be too happy to further your inclinations, my
boy," replied the father. "You certainly appear quite out
of place in your present occupation here.   The house
would have been in ashes but for our timely interference
in building your fire yesterday; the sheep fold was left
open last week and had I not closed the gate in time we
would have been without wool or mutton for the next
five years by the destruction of the whole flock by a score
of famished wolves that are nightly prowling 'round, and
Mary, the milkmaid, says that half the cows yesterday
were turned into pasture without milking, she not being
able alone to milk them."   Then, after a pause, "Yes, I
think a change would be advisable," replied the father.
"But one thing I would most strenuously observe to you:
Beware of the seductive blandishments of those dusky
buxom maidens, far too captivating to the unsophisticated

white man!" "No fear," said the son. "One who has
gone through the firey ordeal of lovely Paris is a living
proof of his safety in this regard." "When do you pro-
pose to start?" said the father. "Not later than Tuesday
next," was the reply. "Well," returned the father, "the
sooner, I think, the better." On the Tuesday following
the sun slowly crept upon the horizon with that peculiar
smoky orange color, denoting the advent of that lovely
genial Indian summer, when nature lavishes in all its
beauty, the comforts to man and the animal creation, the
perfection of its fruits and flowers, with a warning to the
provident tillers of the soil to shield their helpless and
confiding animals from winter's blighting blasts, and
store the well-filled woodshed, destined to feed the glowing embers of the cheerful hearth. It was on the eventful Tuesday the stepson was seen with glowing and smiling countenance, in the garb of a sportsman; his well
laced English walking shoes, surmounted by a pair of
sheepskin gaiters buttoned well up to the knee, the tightly-
fitting corduroy breeches, the capacious waist and shooting coat, replete with roomy pockets, a red flannel shirt

with crimson cravat, a cloth cap with sun-proof peak completed his toilet a la chase. Thus equipped in well-knit frame, gold-rimmed spectacles and his double-barrelled shotgun on shoulder, he looked the type of a London cockney. "Adieu, mon cher pere," he said, extending his hand to his stepfather. "Bon voyage, mon cher fils, et que dieu vous benisse," he replied, and the son left for the Sault Ste. Marie.

After a long and tedious journey overland and by canoe around the devious coast of the Georgian Bay, the channel islands, he arrived at the beautiful island of St. Joseph, on St. Mary's river, sound in limb, to be sure, but worn out with fatigue and privation.

For two days he had scarcely tasted food, excepting the wild raspberries plucked along his path. Carefully lifting his birch canoe over the gravelly beach, he seized a bundle of wild hay from the bottom of his canoe, rolled it up in a bundle, turned over his canoe and coiled himself under it, with the hay for his pillow, and fell sound asleep. How long he remained so he could not tell, but he was awakened by the barking of a dog close by, and

hastily arising from his couch he noticed the dog barking up a tree, and soon observed to his astonishment and
extreme gratification a bevy of partridge, some fifteen or
twenty, scattered about on the limbs of the tree. Seizing his double-barrelled gun he brought two down with
the first shot from the lowest limb, and to his amazement
the rest stood still, while the dog continued barking. He
then took another shot and another couple fell until he
picked out and killed in the same way the whole bevy.

In the meantime the owner of the dog, hearing the
report of guns in rapid succession, hastened to the tree.
She proved to be an old squaw, the mother of the girl
she was leading. She was but a child of fifteen years
and seemed even younger. She wore a neat pair of
deerskin moccasins elaborately embroidered with porcupine quills, these fitting perfectly her well-shaped feet
and ankles, a pair of blue cloth leggins fringed with the
same adorned her limbs, which a loose bright colored
calico gown covered a little below the knee, a broad
leather belt around her well-proportioned waist loosely,
suggesting her maidenly beauty, the curl of her smiling

lip displaying her ivory teeth, her dark gazelle eyes
fringed with long black eyelashes, her raven hair tied on
the back of her neck and falling to her waist, a broad
brimmed straw hat with a wreath of wild roses completed
her island costume. Such did this angelic beauty appear
to this bewildered brain. Addressing the mother, the in-
truder asked, "Cestil l'Isle de St. Joseph?" (is this St. Joseph island)? "Oui, monsieur," replied the dove of fifteen. "Ma mere parl pas Francais." (My mother does
not speak French.) "Can you direct me, my dear, where
I can procure a loaf of bread," he asked her in French.
"Oui, monsieur," she replied, "che nous," (at home).
"And will you allow me to eat in your cabin?" he inquired. "I have tasted no food but wild raspberries for
several days." "Yes," replied the dove, "my mother
says you can, and you are quite welcome."

The stranger was about shouldering his double-barrelled gun and gathering up his wood grouse, when the
dove said, "Permettez moi de vous aider, monsieur, s'il
vous plait," (permit me to help you, sir, if you please),
and this did he cheerfully do. "Avez vous des pomme

de terre?" (Have you potatoes at home) asked the stranger. "Beau coup," (plenty) replied the angel.

"Now I am in luck," thought the stranger, so on arriving at their wigwam, plucking and preparing four of his birds, two for himself and one for each of his guests, he rolled them up separately and folding them up in large basswood leaves buried them in live ashes. They turned out beautifully browned with enough juice to make them relishable, and with a bowl of tea made from the wild teaberry, he dined like a king. As evening approached it was with reluctance that he parted with his entertainers, but with a heavy heart he finally left the beautiful dove and returned to his canoe, to recline his troubled brain on his hay pillow and be lulled to sleep by the plaintive cry of the whip-poor-will. The soft and smoky amber-tinted sun was slowly rising above the blue ethereal horizon when the stranger crept from under his canoe, stripped to the buff and plunged headlong into the limpid waters of this beautiful island and rolling and puffing about like a playful porpoise, struck for shore, and shaking himself like a Newfoundland dog, clothed himself and hied again to the tent of the Indian girl, and to breakfast on ash-roasted wood grouse, corn bread, potatoes and teaberry tea.

A fleet of canoe and Mackinaw boats, containing many of the island Indians, arrived while he was at his breakfast. Their boats were loaded with lake trout and whitefish, which were freely distributed amongst the inhabitants, denoting peace and plenty, and the stranger again realized what his friend St. Martin had told him and he came to this conclusion: "This shall be my home, and the dove my wife, if she will have me," and he asked her, and she replied, "Ask the priest," and he did so, and the priest said, "Make him marry you according to the rules of your church," and under these rules he married her, and at the end of the first year a child was born to the dove, but as time rolled on the fish and game disappeared. It had been a disastrous season and starvation almost stared them in the face. What was to be done? An appeal to his stepfather was the only course, and for him they started. Winter had set in; the earth was mantled in two feet of snow. It was a journey of two hundred and fifty miles on snow-shoes. But the young wife, with her papoose wrapped in a blanket upon her shoulders, followed him. Three weeks elapsed and their journey was accomplished. Exhausted and half starved, with feeble steps they reached the home of his father in the township of Barrie. She waited outside while he entered and approached his parents, who were appalled and thunderstruck at the unexpected return of their prodigal son. "Who is this person who has accompanied and awaits you?" the stepfather demanded. "My wife," he replied. "What? You marry a d—d low-bred squaw, and disgrace yourself and family forever. If you do not leave her, never shall I forgive you; never shall I own you again. Leave her or leave my house at once. Return to your camp, if you choose, but never enter my door again until you give her up." His poor wife had entered the house unobserved, heard this conversation in the adjoining room and quietly raising the window slipped out so gently that she had disappeared from the scene before any further notice was taken of her by the inmates of the house. She had never seriously considered her situation before. The harsh and cruel words of the father rang in her ears. She realized then for the first time what a sacrifice her husband had made, which would ultimately result in the disinheritance if she remained with him, and she determined that, come what might, she would give him up and retrace her steps back to her native isle of St. Joseph, where she would never burden him again. She was all but prostrated with fatigue and hunger; a heavy snow storm was raging; it was late at night, but she never flinched in her purpose for an instant, but tightening the blanket which held her tender babe to her back, she disappeared in the gloom of the storm, turning her steps to the north. Her pride had been trampled under rough-shod heels, but she cast no blame on her husband; neither did she weep or bemoan her own condition. A servant of the house had entered before the stormy interview was over and informed the son that she had gone. "My God," said he, "Gone? Where?" "Why, back to her wigwam," sneeringly replied his father, "the proper place for her." Then continuing the father said, "Once more I ask you to leave this woman for the sake of your family, your interests, your own respectability." "Hush!" said the son. "Not another word; my mind is made up now, if it never was before. This woman is my wife; it was no fault of hers, and I cannot cruelly forsake her and the babe of my own blood to please my family. It is too late now. You can bestow your wealth and position upon someone else. Disinherit me if you choose, but I'm off to overtake my Indian bride. I will never abandon her." And he kept his word, followed and overtook her, and together shared the misery and fatigue of the journey.

Years rolled on and the mother of the dove had secretly known of copper deposits in what is now called the "Bruce mines." The stepson was aware of this and divulged the fact. A company was formed and the result followed of working the mine. He sold out and realized a large sum.

Being well known throughout Ontario, and having moved in his younger days in the best society, his finished education and suavity of manner secured for him a prominent government appointment and he died leaving a large family in civilized life, but not on St. Joseph Island.

--- --- ---

FARMING IN THIS CANADA OF OURS, AND HOW IT WAS I BECAME A FARMER.

When Lasalle and Hennepin, the French explorers, on the 10th of August, 1679, were groping their uncertain way, on the square rigged vessel "Le Griffon" 213 years ago, up the stream from Lake Erie and debouched into the Lake St. Clair, they found it no river at all, and being Frenchmen, they called it in their own language by its proper name, Detroit, that is strait, and named the Indian encampment they had just left the same which it has held till to-day; and on the opposite side just a little below they called it "Les Hurons;" and why? because it was another Indian encampment occupied by that tribe, who cultivated it as other tribes did, along its shores, and when in after years the poor Indians were dispossessed of their cornfields, the Frenchmen took possession, and the first thing they did was to plant pear trees brought from France in groups, and so the shores were ornamented with them. At this late day many of these old French pear trees are still standing, some of them yielding the delicious fruit, but their days will soon be numbered. When John Bull came along and conquered the Frenchmen, he changed the name of "Les Hurons" and called it Sandwich, but that was all he did, for he left them in full possession of their homes, their customs and their religion. It was here I first drew breath on the 30th of April, 1812. In 1816 my father, for his valuable services in the war of 1812, was appointed Inspector General of Upper Canada and moved to Little York (now Toronto) with his family. At that time there were no steamers on the lakes, only small schooners and batteaus. Landing at Chippewa, above the falls of Niagara, a portage was made to Queenston, then by vessel to Little York.

In the year 1819, my father, intent upon giving me the best education in his power, placed me, at an early age, under the tutorship of that remarkable man, Archdeacon

Jock Strachan, as he was irreverently called, and who kept the grammar school in muddy Little York. He was soon succeeded by the Revs. Bethune, Elms, Armour and Phillips. My progress in A, B and C being very slow I was transferred to Mr. Patfield's school. Under the care of this worthy person I first began to feel an interest in my studies, and to him I am indebted (if I may be credited) for writing a legible hand, as also for my slow progress in arithmetic. About this time, 1823, the late Roman Catholic and first bishop of Upper Canada, Alex. McDonnell, of Regiopolis of Glengarry, was making a tour of his diocese, then embracing the whole province of Ontario. This noted pioneer, born at Glenurquhart, Scotland, in 1769, emigrated to Canada with his settlers of one thousand Highlanders and settled there on one hundred and sixty thousand (160,000) acres of land granted by the government in the then wilderness of Glengarry in 1803 and 1804. He was noted for his distinguished services in Canada in the war of 1812 as soldier and chaplain at the battle of Chrystler's Farm on the St. Lawrence, and again at the storming of Ogdensburg in the same year. Died in Dumfries, Scotland, the 14th of January, 1840.

As there was no chapel, much less a church in Little York then, he was a welcome guest in my father's house, whose diningroom served as a chapel for the spare Catholic population of the town and surrounding settlement. A brief sojourn of the bishop led me to form a great reverence for this venerable old pioneer, and his offer to take me in charge as pupil in his new college of St. Raphaels, just opened, was eagerly accepted by my father.

Leaving Little York in the depth of a severe winter, to my youthful imagination, I thought myself singularly favored in having so distinguished an individual as my patron, and luxuriated in the rich fur-robed sleigh that protected me from the keen winter's blast, and driven by his faithful negro valet, Herbert, whose emancipation he had purchased. This journey then from York to St. Raphaels, in Glengarry, involved the necessity of a short visit at all the towns and villages along the travelled road, i. e., Peterboro, Port Hope, Cobourg, Belleville, Prescott and Cornwall. At the last place we tarried for the night with a Mr.

Angus McDonald, if I mistake not the father of the late Premiere, Hon. John Sandfield, of Ontario.

It was during this evening that a few noted persons called to pay their respects to the bishop, and among them was a Miss Ellen Greenfield McDonald, from near St. Raphaels, a great favorite of the bishop's, and who paid me marked attention, I suppose as his companion de voyage.

Unaccustomed as I was to the soothing and kindly influence of ladies' society, having lost my dear mother in my infancy and my sole companions, many of them rude and uncouth playmates; her attention to me was gratifying in the extreme and doubly enhanced my esteem when, in the course of the evening, she was urged to sing, and complying, in the most unaffected and cultivated voice, with thrilling pathos, sang, "Ye Banks and Braes of Bonny Doon," accompanying herself on the harp. On the next day a ride to her home in the bishop's sleigh was offered her and accepted, resulting in my seeing her home, not far from St. Raphaels (his lordship leaving us at his residence). On parting with her she cordially invited me to repeat my visits on holidays, which I was only too glad to do.   There was something so charmingly delightful and attractive in this sweet girl's character that I can never forget the impression she produced upon me, as we stood upon the veranda for the last time, her rich auburn hair ruffled by a gentle breeze, the friendly clasp of her hand, the smile of her dimpled cheek, the sparkle from her lustrous blue eyes, enshrined in the most faultless form of a woman, as she bade me adieu.

How pleasant it was, in after years, to look back to this journey; not alone in making me familiar with the locality of these places, but thrown into society of the most noted families in the province as nothing could exceed the attention and respect paid to this distinguished missionary.   I was not too young to observe a remarkable feature in the state of society through the route I had travelled, for many of the most distinguished were represented by Catholic ladies married to Protestant husbands, and nearly all descendants of U. E. Loyalists.

Ensconced in St. Raphaels, a new phase presented itself to my mind and experience, and I was not a little sur-

prised to learn that I was expected to take care of myself;
that apart from my studies I was to make my bed, sweep
out the sleeping and study room (the brooms made by
ourselves of cedar boughs taken from a swamp hard by),
replenish the water pitchers, clean or black my shoes, and
make a respectable appearance withal; and I conceive no
more salutary practice than this very one, as it taught me
to help myself. My sojourn at St. Raphaels did not produce the result hoped for by my anxious and indulgent
father, for although every attention was paid to moral and
religious training, the education I received was far from fitting me for a profession, owing, more to my dullness than
anything else, I suppose.

A readiness with the pen, however, served a good purpose for the bishop, who put me to the task of copying the
census roll of Glengarry, to form a petition to the government in favor of his new college just started. I was astonished to find that out of one thousand or more names enrolled, ninety-nine out of a hundred were McDonalds or
McDonnells, between which two clans there appeared a
strong rivalry, and the men were distinguished by gallic

nicknames, denoting a long or short nose, or a blue or red one, or by the ears, eyes, complexion or size; but I am sorry to say that I cannot write them down in that beautiful language. What surprised me the most was the stalwart and hardy physique of these Highlanders, for often did they appear at the old St. Raphaels church in their kilts, when we school boys could scarcely keep warm with warm winter clothing. Donald, however, proof against cold in winter in his kilts, was no match for the elephantine truncated mosquitoes in summer, which were to be found in myriads about the Glengarry swamps, as the following incident will prove: Commencing his first summer's residence in Canada, just from Scotland's Grampion Hills, he called upon the Bishop, who asked him how he fared in Canada, and in reply said, "All right, your lordship, but for the infernal mosquitoes, which are devouring me."

"Throw away the kilts then," said the bishop, "and get a pair of buckskin breeches," which he said he would do.

On meeting again his lordship he told him he had followed his advice, but the breeches were not, he had found, proof against the pests, for they pierced him through the buckskin, causing his legs to so swell that he had to rip his breeches up to pull them off. The bishop doubted this, but I believed it, and in after years, to my torture, they have pierced me through a canvas hammock on the shores of the Georgian Bay. .

That these men were loyal, brave, and not over scrupulous, could not be denied. When their services were required to suppress the rebellion in lower Canada in 1838, they went down infantry and returned cavalry, and would have driven home before them the flocks and herds of the rebels, had they been allowed by their superior officers.

Another interesting winter scene to me was the long train (thirty or forty in a string) of traineaus of the habitants loaded with goods from Montreal, where they had been detained by the closing of navigation; and to be taken to the different points in Upper Canada. Let me describe this, if I can: Standing knee deep in snow, and just out of the way of the track, we hear the live tinkling of sleigh bells as merrily approaches the dwarf, hardy Norman bred pony, with the step, strength and agility of a tiger, his shaggy forelock shading his eyes and forehead, and his flowing mane his neck and shoulders, otherwise his coat is as sleek and smooth as that of a mole. On the traineau is a hogshead of sugar seventeen hundred (1,700) pounds in weight, or a hogshead of rum, molasses, or bales of dry goods equal to that weight, but he moves along on his jog trot with the ease of a ship at sea. Following close behind is Jean Baptist, the owner and driver on the same trot, but when tired, steps on the sleigh. He wears the conical bonnet blue, pulled down over his ears, his gray capot and tuque of etoffe du paye (home spun) wound tightly around him, and kept there by a red or blue sash, the bottom of his pants tucked under his socks and lapels of his soulliers de boeuf (half tanned cowhide) well greased and defying snow or rain. The never absent short clay pipe, with its silver tube in which is inserted the bone of a turkey wing, which makes it portable, otherwise carried in his pocket it would break. The strong and fragrant vapors from this fired clay, impregnates the cold and frosty atmosphere and when it is out, he enlivens the air with the stirring song of "A la Clair Fontain" or a "L'omber d'un bois je m'en vais dancer," contented and happy as the day is long and proving the proverb "that where ignorance is bliss, 'tis folly to be wise."

After I had been three years with the worthy bishop he closed his college, I believe for the want of support, his means being very limited, and I returned with him to Toronto, and just at that age when the most important step generally decides the make or break of one pursuit in after life. As already mentioned I was not educated classically, and my inclination led me to a rural life. Intent upon this, I consulted my worthy parent, who had grave and serious objection to that kind of occupation, and he thus reasoned:

"You are unaccustomed to the manual labor that is required in the life of a Canadian farmer, nor are you prepared for the privations, hardships and self-denials involved in such a life, and again you cannot expect to live alone without a helpmate. In all probability you may be blessed with children. Can you imagine the difficulty of raising a family in the back woods, removed from schools, churches, etc? Weigh, then, well the consequences. However, if you have fully made up your mind to follow it, I will give you the choice of a farm in any part of Ontario you may select." I have often thought since what wisdom and plain common sense there was in this wholesome advice. I thought seriously of it and for the time abandoned the idea, but I had left school and something must be done, so I entered a lawyer's office, tried my hand in a grocery store, and at last purchased and sailed a schooner. In February, 1833, my father died, leaving me an ample share of his small fortune, principally in wild lands, and had it been carefully nursed would have left me comfortably provided for in after life, but my old idea for a country life returned, so I took to farming. I had allotted as my share a beautiful farm on the river Thames, two miles above Chatham and containing two hundred and forty-six acres (246) comparatively in a wild state with scarcely any improvements, save a log house and six or eight acres that could be cultivated. I hired a man and his wife to do the housework and commenced chopping and clearing up the land. It was while thus engaged that I met with my first mishap. I had been resting myself after felling a tree and was watching my man cutting through a large one

upon which he was standing, with my right hand resting
on a sapling and nearly within reach of his axe, and as he
was reaching further below the cut, I suddenly felt a sting-
ing pain, and to my consternation found two of my fingers
split to the bone (it was lucky my hand, or my head, for
that matter, was not chopped off, for we were both green
with the axe). Wrapping my fingers up with dead leaves,
we went home, got a bunch of cobwebs in which my
fingers were enveloped and sent for Dr. Ironsides at Chatham, who soon appeared and fastened the fingers together with sticking plaster. It was some time before
I could again shoulder the axe, but quite recovered from
the injury, though the scars are still left. I then began
to realize the truth of my father's admonition, but this did
not intimidate me in the least, and when I recall the first
years of my farming experience it often provokes a smile
at the ridiculous straits I was put to, yet what extraordinary things have been done with this simplest of imple-
ments, and how often from the stately forests, will we see
the change that it will effect in a few short years. In my
short span of life I have witnessed whole townships one

dense mass of forest with swales, swamps and marshes intersecting them in every direction, and the solitary wood-pecker, the drumming partridge, and that king of the fea-thered tribe, the golden crested wild turkey in company with the red deer their sole occupants; and now what do we behold: Commodious and comfortable brick houses and barns, extensive meadows and fields stocked with the finest cattle and sheep in the world, with teeming orchards of the best fruits in America and everything pertaining to the comfort, wealth and edification of a farmer's life adorning their homes; therefore I contend that the sturdy, noble and lion-hearted farmer who has hewed out such a home (and I know thank Providence, many of them) is as equally deserving of a crown, and far more so, than the greatest heroes of the age.

In pursuing this secluded life deprived of all amuse-ments, the greatest pleasure is to make the most of your surroundings, and rejoice in the successful efforts in sub-duing the stately forests, and witnessing the vigorous growth of your first crops from the virgin soil, and pleased to make of your patient ox and faithful steed your constant companions in labor, and their only reward meted out to them by gentle treatment and care for their comforts. The fruits of your labors should afford you innnite pleasure, as you observe the thrifty orchard, and well stocked vegetable garden, supplying you with delicious fruits and vegetables, and what with the ornamental trees judiciously laid out and beautifying your country home, what more could one reasonably desire. To bring this about, however, cannot be accomplished without ceaseless toil, excessive labor and patience, or abundant means (money) to employ others to do it. Not being inured by practice in the days of my youth to the former, and not possessing the latter, I struggled along.

I will now return to my first straits. I think about the greatest difficulty I had to contend with was the making of bread; as we had no cooking stoves in those days, the old-fashioned Dutch oven (simply an iron pot with a cover) was the sole one in use, but as only one loaf at a time could be baked, it was exceedingly troublesome, so I determined to build a clay one, such as were seldom seen, and originated with the first and probably French or Dutch

settlers, and as a neighbor of mine had some little knowledge of their construction, I secured his services. So we
went to work and sank four posts in the ground, four feet
high, and across the top of these we laid split puncheons
or staves of bass wood to form a bed or foundation, say
four by six feet, over which it was to be covered with eight
inches of mortar, or clay, then we took an empty barrel
with the head knocked out, and laid it on its side length-
ways. Now this was to form the shape of the oven, then
we commenced preparing the mud cats. My readers, I am
sure, never heard of that name. Well, I will tell you
what they were, and how made. We made a hole in the
ground, throwing the top soil away, and came to the clay,
which we had worked up with the spade and hoe, to the
consistency of thick mortar, then a hay rope about two
feet long and size of your thumb, which we souced and
worked in this mortar until it was about as thick as your
arm, then laid it carefully around the barrel and over it; this
is a mud cat. Leaving a place for the door and shaping it
the size you want it with a piece of hoop iron; then we give
it a thick coat of mortar, making it about eight inches

thick—behold the oven built. Now we fill the barrel chock full of kindling and set it on fire, and when it is burned out your work is done, and I'll wager there is no invention of man that will equal it in turning out a batch of bread, pumpkin or apple pie, roast pig, turkey or beef. Regarding this oven business, as everything must be economized to make a successful farmer it has led to all the improvements of the age, and the saving of labor has been the first consideration. Now, when my oven was built I had not taken a wrinkle from my good friend and neighbor, Jake Shepley, and if "an honest man is the noblest work of God" he was one, but he did away with the hoe and spade to a great extent, as I will try and explain. Going to Jake's one fine day I found him seated by the side of a pit which he had dug out, with a pail of water on one side and a half bushel measure of peas on the other and six thundering barrows (hogs) in the pit. I saluted him thus: "Jake, what in Sam Hill are you doing?" Squirting a mouthful of tobacco juice clear over the pit he replied, "I am preparing for mud-cats." He then threw in a handful of peas, then a bucket of water,

"MAKING MUD CATS."

and the way those hogs went at it was "root hog or die;" and thus he prepared clay for his oven. Nothing like necessity, the mother of invention.

About this time I had a visit from my neighbor, John Arnold, who asked me to ride with him to Chatham, when the following conversation took place: "Well, Mr. B., how do you like farming?" "I rather like the country life," I replied, "but I don't think there is much money in it." "You are right," he said, "there is not. Keep out of debt, economize and utilize all you can. Now, I think," he continued, "that you labor under great disadvantages, and I'll tell you what I mean. You are lucky in getting your farm without paying for it, but you have to pay out money for all you touch; for instance, you paid for your horses, wagon, harness, plough, etc., and even your hats, coats, shirts, boots and socks and everything you have. That is your case. Now here is mine. Father gave me my lot and an old mare and cow, and after a few years I had enough land cleared to keep a dozen sheep. On my father's farm we were four or five boys and as many girls and brought up to all kinds of work. On the farm was a blacksmith and carpenter shop, and we were taught all kinds of work on rainy days; to make or repair a wagon wheel, make a bull-plough (made entirely of wood, and faced with a plate of steel. They lasted for years in the clay soil of Kent, where there are no stones.) I raised my horses from the old mare, and made my wagon, plough and harrow. The harness, a breast strap and rope traces, and no britchen required, as there are no hills. My hat a straw," he continued, "is made by my daughters; my coat, pants and shirts are home made; even my shoe packs I made myself out of a hide that Peter Ralston, alias 'Peter Rawhide,' tanned on shares; and my harness the same. Now all I have to pay for is a pound of tea a month for the old woman; I don't buy any sugar, for I have a sugar bush and make lots of sugar to sell." Now here was a lesson for me, and it reminds me now of another instance of a successful farmer who settled on the shores of Lake Simcoe many years ago, and who came to Canada from England with some ten or fifteen thousand pounds sterling, and purchased four hundred acres in a block there. He brought with him his young wife, just married, an accomplished and highly educated person. After cleaning up a hundred acres or so and building commodious barns and beautifying his forest home, his poor wife, suffering from the great wants and privations attending so secluded and laborious a life, sickened and died. Plunged in the deepest affliction at this irreparable loss, he tried to sell out and leave Canada, but was dissuaded from it, in fact he had spent so much of his means that no purchaser could be found. Knowing the inutility of farming without a wife, and not disposed to marry again, except an English lady, he went to England and brought out another one, equally accomplished as the first, and lo! in a few years she passed away as did the previous one. It was at this period that my informant called upon him and found him in a state of frenzy, crushed by his dire misfortunes and resolved to quit the country forever, but he had spent so much improving his place that again no purchaser could be found. In this state he left him, and when my informant paid him the next visit, a few years after, he found him in his harvest field with several loaded wagons securing a bountiful crop of one hundred acres of wheat, joyous, happy and contented. "Why," he remarked, "Mr. S., you appear in a very different mood than when I last saw you." "Yes," he replied, "then I was crushed indeed, but time has its soothing influence and finding that I could not sell out except at a ruinous sacrifice I determined to take another wife. She is to the manor born, inured to the climate, familiar with all the duties of a backwoods life, makes our own clothes, goes to market and provides for the house with sales of butter, poultry, eggs, etc., and we are making money hand over fist." How many similar cases have I known in Canada, but how few succeeded as well in a pecuniary way.

Now came the tug of war—plowing. I had a pretty good span of horses, but they were as strange to the plow as I was, who never handled one. I was then twenty-four years old. They were in good order, fat, frisky and playful, and I was strong, active and fearless. I had opened two or three furrows around the field (instead of in lands, ten or twelve feet wide, the proper way) and following the plow and horses sometimes at a trot, the sweat pouring from my face and the horses in a lather, when an extraordinary sensation seized me, as if some fiend had brained me with a club. Recovering from my stupor I found myself straddle of the beam of the plow, and the horses out of sight. The plow had struck a hidden root, the double tree had parted in the middle and the lines around my neck jerked me suddenly over the handles and onto the beam. Limp and sore I found my poor horses at the stable door, who saluted me with a snort. Patting them gently I led them back to the plow. Do you think that that intimidated me? No, but still I could not forget my poor father's counsel. I learned afterwards to hold the lines in each hand and not around my neck, and thus avoid another thunder clap.

It was not only with the plow that I found myself astray, but in a thousand other things. Laboring then under these serious disadvantages I struggled along for want of being educated in the mysteries of a farmer's life; for though ever so simple, they are as necessary to learn and master, as is Blackstone to the advocate, Abernethy to the physician, Watts to the engineer, or belles letters to the philosopher.

It was while intent and determined to follow this pursuit in life, that I took to myself a partner, and although unaccustomed to life in the backwoods, she cordially and cheerfully aided me in my every effort—but man proposes and God disposes—alas, in nine months on a tempestuous and stormy night in February she passed away, leaving a still born infant as a pledge of our love.

My hearth and home became too desolate, and I left it to allow the current of time to allay the troubled stream, and after a four years' respite again took another partner, and lo, the avenger cleft from my side another flower of Eve. Many would suppose that this was enough to discourage me, but no, such are the attractions of "Home, sweet Home," that it is difficult to part with the shade trees that you have planted to screen the rays of the meridian sun from the cottage door, the thrifty fruit trees that have contributed their luscious fruits to appease the thirsty palate, and the creeping rose and honeysuckle perfuming the air that invites you to repose. Again did the third partner link her fate to mine. Nurtured and accustomed to the refinements and luxuries of a city life, attractive by her charms, she forsook all to share my lot.

The privations, exposure and hardships of her forest home preyed upon her health, and as if to crown all our misfortune in the depth of a cold winter night, with two feet of snow mantling the earth, a blaze was discovered in the roof of the house, and in the space of one short hour all was swept as by a tornado, and our child of two years old was with difficulty snatched from the devouring flames. Did this even intimidate me? By no means. On the very spot where lay the ashes of my once happy home another was erected, of far more commodious and comfortable proportions, but for various reasons I abandoned it to cast my lot in a different sphere of life without a regret, for events have proved to me that I struck a wrong track when I took to farming, and I am reminded of a jocular remark made to me by my old friend, John Prince, who, when he first came to Canada in 1832, said, "my father kept a pack of hounds in England, but they soon ate him up." Now in comparing my lot to his there was but this difference, the hounds did not consume me, but my farm did, and I would certainly advise any young man or old one (if he desires to farm in Canada), to apprentice himself to a prosperous and practical farmer and acquire a thorough knowledge of it before launching on so precarious a sea of life.

In 1858 I bade farewell to my forest home with mingled feelings of pleasure and regret, and a broad field of uncertainty before me, but the active life I had led unsuited me for a sedentary one, and I was soon induced to embark in a trade, which unfortunately proved as disastrous quite, if not more so, than farming for want of knowledge and experience, for in the former the loss came by slow degrees, whereas in the latter it came with a running hop, skip and a jump. Need I say it was the trade of tanning. Not having the slightest experience in the matter, I had to trust entirely to others. I started in an old tannery, with vats filled with old liquor (extract of tan bark which had lost its strength for several years standing), but used by my ignorant foreman with fresh liquor. Consequently, hides and skins to the value of thousands of dollars were turned out, after six months' anxious waiting, almost worthless. The reverse was apparent, I was tanned, instead of the leather. I never recovered from this false step sufficiently to continue in this trade, so left it with dear bought experience. The great Napoleon wisely said, "C'est le premier pas qui cout." The first step, wisely or unwisely taken, leads to success or failure, or in other words, "There is a time and tide in the affairs of men; if taken at the ebb, leads on to fortune." I always struck it at the wrong time. Resting on my oars at this juncture, a bait was thrown out to me by a friend that I eagerly seized, which was to open a stone quarry on the Great Manitoulin Island. The enterprise ended in forming a company to bore for oil instead, and after expending $50,000 of the company's money 100 barrels only was pumped out, and with it my last dollar. So ended that venture.

A northerly current drifted me into the regions of Lake Michigan and Green Bay in the service of the United States Lake Surveys of the Racine Reef and locating the present Sturgeon Bay ship canal. Too much praise cannot be said in favor of the discipline, order and efficiency of this admirable corps. After an honorable discharge from this service I struck the Great Western Railway, and at last came to anchor in H. M. Customs at Windsor, from whence it is not likely I will be ever able to hoist sail for another port.

TWENTY-TWO YEARS' SERVICE IN H. M. CUS-
TOMS.

———

In assuming the duties of this office I was assured by those in authority that so long as I was able to discharge the duties of it I would not be disturbed, but in this I was mistaken, as the following epistle will show:

Sir—I have it in command to acquaint you that His Excellency, the Governor-General in Council, has been pleased to place you on the retired list, to take effect from the 12th day of July, 1895, with an allowance at the rate of $308 00 per annum—viz., $25 66 per month.   I have the honor to remain, sir,   Your obt. servant,

S. M. McMICHAEL,

Acting Commissioner.

Ottawa, July 27, 1895.

Did those good people in Ottawa consider for one moment the painful and humiliating position of placing an old and faithful servant of twenty-two years' service and 83 years of age with an invalid wife on the paltry pension of $25 66 per month? No, they did not. They were misinformed, as some of them acknowledged afterwards; but the mischief was done and no remedy. Hence the production of these memoirs, from necessity.

The experience of so many years spent at this port, the most important in the Dominion as regards the traffic between the two countries, requires greater vigilance than at any other in it, and whatever I have to say about it can do no harm to anybody and may interest a few. At the imminent risk of giving grave offense to my Canadian friends, I would venture the opinion that taking a leaf from Uncle Sam would be advisable. Why not clothe landing waiters in uniform? It was proposed some years ago, but fell through. As punctuality, obedience and promptness to duty are considered requisite in all matters of business, the inexperienced and raw recruit (a landing waiter) often finds himself at fault in his onerous duties, and requires the constant care and solicitude of his superior officer. When practicable it is desirable having landing waiters, at ferries particularly, conversant with both languages. As an instance: A buxom, dashing young lady landed with a two-story Saratoga trunk and a yearling tot. When she was asked to examine it, no answer. Where bound? Still no answer. "Parlez vous Francais?" I asked her. "Oh, oui, monsieur," she replied. I found out she was going to a station on the C. P. R. R. "How much money have you?" I asked. "One dollar and fifty cents," she replied. If she hired a hack to take her and trunk to the station, they would charge her $1; so I hired a spring dray for twenty-five cents, sat her and tot on the trunk and she left satisfied. Three or four days after a Frenchman (her brother) appeared and presented me with a six-pound dressed turkey, thanking me for the little trouble I had taken. The straits that innocent people to avoid customs are put to is often pitiable. A handsome and attractive brunette was asked to show what was in her basket (a loose towel rolled up in it), but sad to relate, in stooping to do so the end of a six-pound rump steak was exposed at the end of her shawl, which she had suspended from a string tied round her shoulders. What could the officer do but tell her to conceal it better the next time, and allow her to pass on? A little attention to strangers is proper.

Seated on the veranda at the British American, a lady sat near me with her three romping children tumbling about her. I knew she was from Galveston, Tex. I ventured to remark that she must find it troublesome to travel alone. "Excepting," she said, "to pass through those horrible customs, I have no trouble. I leave for New York this evening to join my husband, a fancy dry goods merchant at Galveston." "You assure me," I answered, "that you have not purchased anything in Canada." "Certainly not," she replied. "You can satisfy yourself." Which I did. I then told her I would accompany her with her trunks across the river and try to help her. Accompanying her to Detroit, I approached the United States landing waiters, whom I have always found civil and obliging, and I said to them, "Gentlemen, this is a lady from one of your cities. I am satisfied she has bought nothing in Canada. Here are the keys of her trunks," handing them to them, "if you desire to open them." "If you assure us that it is so, Mr. B—," was the reply, "she can

pass on." She had them checked to New York and returned to dine at the American, and would take the train in
the afternoon.   On leaving the hotel she expressed the ob-
ligation she felt for the little trouble I had taken.   I begged
to assure her that I was paid by H. M., the Queen, for all I
did, and she would feel highly offended if she thought her
servants did not always acquit themselves properly.   "May
you, then, always smoke the pipe of peace between the two
countries," she remarked, at the same time handing me a
beautiful meershaum pipe in a case.

A poor woman came off the boat with a basket containing articles of clothing, shoes, socks and scraps of calico,
amounting to about $2.   I told her they were dutiable, and
she replied she had not a cent left.   I asked her to accompany me to the collector, and he would act in the manner
he thought proper.   Her husband rented a small piece of
land in Anderdon.   He had been bed-ridden for three years
past; she had six children, all young; had worked all winter
making straw braid, with the light of a chimney fire; no
sale for it in Windsor; had to sell it in Detroit, and ex-

changed it for these goods. She was allowed to go, and felt much relieved and thanked the collector (Mr. Benson).

Such were a few of the many incidents encountered in this most thankless and disagreeable occupation, relieved in a great measure by the kind and courteous feelings existing with the officers composing the Windsor staff and the public as well.

William Lewis Baby   Frontispiece

De Stack was good for him, and De Blanket Too   27

An Interrupted Supper   31

Mending his Trousers   33

Hon. James Baby Inspector General   58

Col. John Prince   97a

Old Baby House at Sandwich Ontario   116

Chippewa Creek   124

He went at them with the will of a Tiger   138

He was badly frostbitten   140

Who and what the devil are you   146

An Indian Bride   224

Making Mud Cats   256

Abbott, James: 15
Airey, Col.: 92, 93, 110, 112,
Alan, William: 12a.
Aljoes: 123a
Allen, Van: 99
Ambridge, Major: 78
Amherstburg: 78, 79, 85,
119a, 124, 129
Anderdon Township: 270a
Anderson, General: 81, 89
Andrew (Slave):132, 133,
134, 135, 136, 137,138
Armour, Rev.: 242
Arnold, John: 257
Assumption Church: 127a
Astor, John Jacob: 15
Bâby Mansion: 117, 118, 119,
129, 130, 131, 138, 159
Bâby & Hanrahan's Liquer
Store: 2
Bâby, Baptiste: 159
Bâby, Charles: 12b, 25, 26,
100, 122a, 126a, 129, 133,
134, 135, 137, 138, 139, 140,
150, 159, 162, 210
Bâby, Francois: 5, 14, 91a, 93,
101, 111, 210
Bâby, George: 210
Bâby, Horace: 210
Bâby, Jacque Duperon:1, 3, 4,
6, 7, 8, 9, 10, 11
Bâby, James: 45, 52, 55, 58,
59, 60, 64, 70, 151
Bâby, Raymond: 12b, 12d
Baker, Tyas: 104

Baptist, Jean: 249
Batner, Father: 168, 174
Bear's Rump Island: 192
Bell, Captain: 75, 76, 93, 100,
101
Belle (Hog) Island: 1, 7, 107,
111, 216
Belleville: 243
Bennett, Mr.: 105, 109
Benson, Mr.: 271a
Bethume, Re;v.:242
Birse, General: 103
Black Hawk, Chief: 82
Black;, Mr. 99
Bois Blanc: 78
Bolton, -----: 57
Bondhead, Sir Francis: 50, 74
Boulton, Hon. I.H.: 12c
Brady, General: 94, 95, 96,
112
Brantford: 41
Brenman, Rev.: 127a
Brereton, Patrick: 72
British American Hotel
(Pierre St. Amour's Inn): 144,
269a
Brock, Sir Isaac: 51, 57, 90a,
91a, 92a, 93a, 96a, 130
Broderick, Capt.: 109, 111,
113
Brooker's Inn: 77
Brophy, Captain: 81, 83, 84,
88, 89
Brown, Mr.: 221
Bruce Mines: 224, 239

Bucket, Capt. Bill: 123
Buchanan, Mr.: 41
Buffalo: 44, 45, 77, 125, 128
Bull, John: 241
Bullock's Tavern: 79
Burford Woods: 123a
Campbell, Sir Alexander: 185, 186
Campbell, W.: 12c
Campion, Rev.:127a
Canada Company: 38
Canadian Correspondent Newspaper: 71
Canadian Pacific Railroad: 268a
Canadian Southern Railroad: 35
Canard Bridge: 119a
Cape Smith: 187, 219
Caron, Francois: 14
Cartier, Claude. 76, 140, 141, 142, 145
Cass, John: 24
Cass St. Detroit: 15
Chatham:18, 20, 24, 26, 34, 42, 43, 72, 75, 76, 86, 115, 118, 140, 142, 251, 252, 257
Chauvan, Francois: 18, 19, 20
Chewett, Capt.: 110
Chicago: 194, 214
Chippewa: 118, 124, 125, 241
Chone, Father: 168
Chrysler, H.: 24
Chrysler's Farm: 57, 128a, 242

Clark's Dock: 162,
Cleveland, City of: 126, 133, 181
Clinton, Captain W.R.: 77, 94a
Cobourge: 243
Colburne, Sir John: 50, 74
Colchester: 125
Cole, Mr.: 105
Collingwood: 166, 215,
Colonial Advocate Newspaper: 12b, 43, 46
Cooper, -----: 12a, 35
Cornwall: 243
Credit River: 122
Crooks, Hon. James: 123a
Cullan, Rev.: 127a
Dauphin, Narcisse: 24, 76
Davis, Captain: 87, 89
Dearborn: 75
Delaware Township: 163
Denison, Col. George: 123
Dennison, Mr: 109
Detroit: 2, 13, 15, 18, 51,5 7, 59, 75, 85, 91, 94, 95, 96, 99, 102, 105, 112, 115, 120a, 117, 118, 130, 132, 138, 159, 163, 181, 240, 270a
Detroit Public Library: 159
Detroit River: 1, 2, 14, 16, 37, 60, 121a, 124a, 117, 120, 131, 162, 215, 216
Dixon, Capt.: 89a, 91a, 92a,
Dodge, Col.: 81, 83, 84, 88, 89

Don River: 122, 157
Dougall, James: 41, 42, 77, 93, 100, 106
Dorchester Woods: 144, 145
Duffield, Professor: 181
Dundas: 122a
Dunkirk Lighthouse: 127
Durham, Lord: 51
Eagle Tavern: 128
Edward, Albert: 95a, 97a
Elliott, Capt.: 99, 100, 101, 102, 108
Elliott, Charles: 109, 114
Elliott, Mathew: 89, 91a, 93a
Elliott's Point:, 79, 80, 81
Elms, Rev.: 242
Essex County: 13, 46
Evans, Isreal: 24
Ewert, J. B.: 123a
Farrel, Bishop: 174
Ferrar, Father: 168
Field & Cahoon: 121
Fighting Island: 78, 85
Forsyth, Major: 94
Fort Erie: 9,56
Fort Gratiot Road: 94
Fort Niagra: 158
Fort Pontchartrain: 2
Fort Shelby: 91a, 93a
Fort William: 183
Fox, Capt.: 92, 99, 100, 101
Fox, John: 125, 126, 127
Galveston Texas: 269a
Gardener's (Gardner's) Mill Dam: 42, 123a

Gardner & Babcock Store: 106
Georgeon Bay: 166, 183, 185, 216, 219, 223, 229, 232, 248
Gidly, Capt.: 216
Gignac, Mr.: 85
Girty: Prideax: 124
Gladwin, Major: 6, 7, 8, 9, 11, 12
Glascow, Captain: 86'
Glengerry Woods: 242, 246
Goderich: 218, 219, 223
Gorden, James: 79
Gordon, Rev.: 127a
Gorden River: 220
Gore Bay: 222
Gosfield Township: 121, 124
Goyeau, Daniel: 14
Great Western Railroad: 20, 34, 94a, 166, 266
Green Bay: 117, 209, 265
Griswold Street Detroit: 2, 15
Grosse Point: 216, 217
Hagerman,?: 56
Hall, W.G.: 78, 80
Hamilton (City): 18, 174
Hands, Felix: 13, 14, 16, 23, 28, 30, 31, 32, 33, 34
Hands, William: 13
Hanepeau, Father: 168, 176, 185
Harris, John: 42
Harrison, Gen.: 119, 130
Harsen's Island: 218
Harvell, Mr.: 102

Harwich Township: 27
Hebert, Rev. F.J.: 183, 184
Hennepin: 240
Heward, Charles: 12b
Hiram Walker: 216
Hotel Diew Hospital: 121a
Hotel Iroquois: 222
Howard Township: 27, 34
Hudson Bay Company: 14, 185
Hull, Gen. 119, 130
Humber River: 122, 123
Hume, Doctor: 104, 105, 106
Huron, Indians (Village): 10, 79, 240
Ingersoll's Inn: 123a
Ironside, George Dr.: 110, 252
Isle of Caves: 219
Jack O Lantern (in sky): 126
Jackson, Andrew: 73
Jacobs, George: 116a
James, Harry:20
James, Samuel: 114
Janette's Creek: 21,23
Jannette, Francois: 98, 101
Jarvis, Samuel: 12c
Jarvis St. Toronto: 12a
Jeannette, Charles: 14
Jesuit Pear Trees: 120, 241
Jesuit Priests: 168
Johnson, William: 111, 114
Jonathon, C.: 29, 30, 32, 34, 35
Jones, H.J.: 57, 75

Kelly, Purser: 218
Kent County: 13, 46, 78, 85, 86, 258
Kentucky, State of: 132, 134, 135, 136
Killarney: 166, 174, 181, 185, 187, 188, 215
King George III of England: 4
King George IV of England: 38
King, James: 12b, 12c, 12d
Kingston: 125a
Kincardine: 219
Kirby House: 194
Kirkpatrick, John: 124
Kohler, Father: 168
Labalaine, Francis: 14, 15
Laframboise: 10
Lafrance, Pierre: 169, 170, 171, 172, 173
Lake Erie: 9, 118, 119, 126, 148, 151, 240
Lake George: 220
Lake Huron: 120, 154, 172, 183, 216, 218, 229
Lake Michigan: 265
Lake Ontario: 124, 158
Lake St. Clair: 1, 16, 18, 77, 114, 124a, 216, 217, 240
Lake Simcoe: 258
Lake Superior: 120, 164, 183, 185, 229
Lamarandier, Charles: 167
Lampton County: 13,46
Langlois, Pierre: 17

LaSalle: 240
Latraverse, 15
Laughlin, Major: 79
Lawler, Rev.: 127a
LeGriffon: 240
Leighton, H.: 80
Leslie, Capt.: 100
LeValle's Point: 16
Lewis, Capt.: 92, 93, 94, 95, 97, 98, 99, 100
Lewis, Mr. Ira: 223
Littibache, F. (Inn): 124a
London, City: 42, 84, 85, 92, 163
Long Woods: 123a, 146
Lossing's Life of George Washington Book: 194, 197, 201, 208
Lundy's Lane: 55
MacKenzie, William Lyon: 12a, 12b, 12d, 43, 74, 75
Mackinac: 117
Mackinac Toast: 3
Maidstone: 119a
Maillioux, Mr.: 100
Maitland, Lady Sarah: 149
Maitland River: 218
Maitland, Sir Peregrine: 50, 148
Malden Township: 91, 92, 93, 94, 97, 106, 115
Malory, Capt.: 125a
Manitoulin Island: 164, 167, 187, 219, 222, 265
Manitowoning: 219

Marrantete, Mr.: 94
Martin (Indian): 113
Mason, Tom: 78
McAuley, Sir J.B.: 55
McCrae, W.: 24
McCree, T.: 76
McCreedy: 125
McDonald, Angus: 56, 244
McDonald, Ellen Greenfield: 244
McDonell, Rev, Angus: 127a,
McDonell, Rev. W.P.: 127a
McDonnell, Judge: 95, 96
McDonnell, Alex Bishop: 242
McDougall, Peter: 12c
McGregor, Duncan: 99
McGregor's Saw Mill: 118
McKay, Mate: 216
McKenzie, Capt. R.N.: 125a
McLean, ----: 56
McMichael, S.M.: 266a
McNab, ----: 57
McNabb, Sir Allan: 74
Menominee Bridge: 212
Mercer, Robert: 93, 114
Miconce, Joe (Indian): 187, 188, 190, 191, 192
Michigan, State of: 135
Mills, Mr.: 98
Milwaukee: 193
Mohawk Indians: 81
Montgomery's Tavern: 74
Montreal: 75, 118, 210, 248
Moravian Town: 92a, 123a, 163

Morse, Mr.: 104, 105
Mosa: 42, 123a
Muncy Town (Indian
Village): 163
Navy Island: 44, 74, 75
New York: 269a, 270a
Niagra: 44, 74, 125a,
Niagra River: 118, 120, 124,
125, 209, 241
Northern Railroad: 166
Oats, Capt. R.: 123
O'Connell, Dan: 117a
O'Flaherty, Patrick: 196, 197,
198, 199
O'Grady, Rev. W.T.: 70
Ogdenburg: 55, 242, 243
Ohio, State of: 132
Olinda, Iron Furnace: 121
Oswego: 55
Ottawa City of: 185, 266a
Ottawa Indians: 5
Otterbury, Mr. 98
Ouellette, Vital: 14
Oxford's Corners: 123a
Parent, Jacques: 17
Park Farm: 116a, 119a
Patfield's School: 242
Payne, Major: 94, 112
Peche (Peach) Island: 1, 216
Pelette, Alexis: 96, 97
Pensylvania: 182,
Perrier, James: 22, 72, 73
Peterborough: 243
Phillips, Rev.: 242
Pierre St. Amour's Inn (British

American Hotel): 144, 269a
Point Abino: 125, 126
Pontiac, Chief : 1, 2, 3, 5, 7,
82
Port Arthur: 221
Port Dalhousie: 124
Port Hope: 243
Port Robinson: 124
Port Talbot: 150,
Pottanattomie, Indians: 10
Pratt, Dominique: 17
Pratt, Francois: 14
Prescott: 243
Prince, Col. John: 79, 82, 83,
84, 92, 93, 99, 100, 102, 103,
105, 106, 107, 108, 109, 110,
111, 113, 114, 116, 116a,
118a, 151, 152, 263
Proctor, Col.: 119
Proudfoot, I.: 12c
Puce River: 1
Putnam, Mr.: 102
Quebec. City of: 63. 84, 135,
182, 210
Queenstown: 74, 118, 241
Radcliff, Col.: 78, 79, 80, 89
Raleigh Rd.: 34
Raleigh Township: 141, 145
Ralston, Peter: 258
Rankin, Author: 119a, 120a,
121a
Rankin, Charles.: 102, 107,
120a
Rankin House: 140
Rathbun, Ben: 128

Read, James: 76, 92
Reaume, Susanne (Mrs. Jaques Bâby) 3, 4, 6, 62
Renfrew, Baron: 95a
Retter, Mr.: 98
Richardson, Charles: 12c, 158
Ridge Road: 27
Ridgetown: 27, 29
Ridley, Joe: 125, 126
River Canard: 10
Robinson, Sir John Beverly: 49, 52, 54
Rogers, J.: 194, 214
Rudyard, Captain: 89
Sacketts Harbour: 125a
Sailing Ship Captain Bill Bucket: 125a
Sailing Ship Captain John McIntosh: 125a
Sailing Ship Kingston Packet: 125a
Sailing Ship Tecumseh:124, 127
Sailing Ship The Brothers: 125a
Sandwich Towne: 13, 16, 17, 25, 34, 37, 40, 51, 63, 89a, 91, 92, 94, 96, 99, 103, 104, 105, 106, 108, 110, 113, 115, 116, 116a, 117a, 121a, 122a, 124a, 127a, 117, 121, 129, 131, 152, 159, 163, 164, 181, 210, 241
S & W Streetcar: 89a
Sandfield, Hon. John: 244
Shepley, Jake: 256

Sloop Duke of Richmond: 125a
Sloop Captain Richard Oats: 125a
Smith, Capt.: 223
South Bay: 164
Southampton: 219
St. Armour, Pierre: 14
St. Clair River: 13, 115, 154, 218
St. Joseph's Island: 222, 232, 234, 238, 240
St. Lawrence River: 242
St. Mary's River: 215, 220, 229, 232
St. Paul Min.: 117
St. Raphaels College: 243, 244, 245, 246, 247
St. Thomas: 148,150,152
Sarnia: 13, 15, 97a, 144, 145, 218
Sault Ste. Marie: 14, 16, 117, 166, 215, 220, 222, 229, 232
Schneider: 33, 35
Schooner Ann: 79, 80, 87
Shelby St. Detroit: 15
Sherwood,-----: 56
Shover's Inn: 77
Sloop, Duke of Richmond: 123
Smith, -----: 89
Southwest Fur Company: 15
Sparke, Capt.: 92, 99, 100, 101, 102, 104, 115
Split Log, Chief: 91a, 92a,

130
Steamer Alciopie: 125a
Steamer Am.: 125a
Streamer Cambria: 215, 219
Steamer Canada: 157
Steamer Caroline: 44, 45, 74
Steamer Capt. Whitney: 125a
Steamer Champlain: 95, 96
Steamer Emerald: 125
Steamer Empire: 221
Steamer Frontinac: 125a
Steamer General Brady l: 78
Streamer Great Britain: 125a
Steamer Kingston Bucket:
123
Steamer Martha Ogden: 125a
Steamer Ontario: 125a
Steamer Queenston: 125a
Steamer Windsor: 94a, 95a
Steamboat Thames: 99
Steam Ferry United: 77
Stoney Point: 17, 77
Strachan, James: 12d, 46, 48,
55, 57
Strachan, John (Archdeacon):
241, 242,
Street, Thomas: 125
Sturgeon Bay Ship Canal: 265
Sumner, V.: 72
Talbot, Col.: 38, 149, 150,
151, 152, 153
Talbot (Brother of the Col.):
148
Tecumseh, Chief: 82, 90a,
91a, 92a, 93a, 130

Templeton, Mr.:222
Thames River: 19, 24, 25, 27,
29, 42, 72, 123a, 124a, 130,
140, 163, 251
Thayer, ——: 89
Thebo, Capt.: 92, 99, 100, 101
Theller, Doctor: 75, 78, 81,
82, 83, 84
Theresa (Negress): 3, 10
Tober, Mary: 223
Toronto (York): 17, 25, 40,
41, 43, 44, 47, 49, 52, 54, 63,
74, 120a, 122a, 124a, 125a,
128a, 121, 124, 140, 141, 144,
145, 148, 151, 156, 158, 159,
162, 163, 166, 182, 226, 241,
242, 243, 250
Townsend, Major: 85
Traveler's Home Inn: 146
Turkey Island: 11,12
Underground Railroad: 132
United Empire Loyalists: 37,
50, 51, 57, 86, 155, 245
Upper Canada Bank: 157
Vanallan, Capt: 125
Vantrampe, Jules: 199
Vidal, Capt.: 141, 144, 145,
154
Walpole Island: 120a, 218
Ward, Artemus: 97a
Watson, John G.: 14
Welland Canal: 49,124
Wickwimilong Village: 167,
174, 183, 219
Widmer, Doctor: 145

Windsor: 14, 34, 41, 75, 77, 78, 85, 94a, 91, 93, 96, 97, 99, 100, 102, 103, 106, 107, 110, 111, 112, 120A, 144, 166, 215, 223, 266, 270a, 271a
Whithead's Inn: 123a
Wood, W.R.: 100, 121a
Woodward Ave. Detroit: 15,96a
Woodworth, Ben: 94, 95
Wyandotte, Indians: 5, 10
Young Men's Library: 193
Young St. Toronto: 12a

www.ingramcontent.com/pod-product-compliance
Lightning Source LLC
Chambersburg PA
CBHW032030090426
42733CB00029B/75